A Book of Golf

BY

J. BRAID, J. A. T. BRAMSTON,
H. G. HUTCHINSON, &c.

EDITED BY

E. F. BENSON
and
E. H. MILES

Illustrated with Photographs by A. Gandy, Winchester.

NEW YORK
E. P. DUTTON & CO.
31, West Twenty-Third Street
1903

PREFACE.

THE careful reader will, it is hoped, in the ensuing pages find many mutually contradictory rules laid down for his guidance, and if this book is to be of any profit, this must be so. For though twice two is invariably four, though the ace of trumps invariably takes the trick, though if one's head is cut completely off one invariably dies, the goddess of golf soars untrammelled above those very dull things known as rules without exceptions. True, like a balloon, she casts a grappling-iron to earth when she practically tells everybody to keep his eye on the ball, but in the main the perfect freedom of her service allows, nay, commands, the worshipper to perform his strokes of homage in the method that to him comes easiest.

Thus, James Braid, an arch-druid indeed, does not use the same ritual as Mr. J. A. T. Bramston; the Braid-use differs in many respects from the Bramston-use, yet both—as anyone who has witnessed knows—are absolutely right. The third arch-druid, again, Mr. H. G. Hutchinson, in practice certainly differs from both, but to say he was wrong would merely be to confess that one does not know what golf is. The use for parents and guardians, again, differs from all the others so much that at first sight it looks like a different creed. Yet if parents and guardians were to adopt the Braid-use, they would be guilty of a greater heresy. They would also immediately spoil many new and valuable golf balls.

The devout worshipper, then, finds himself in a difficulty: the Braid-use gives certain rubrics, the Bramston-use not only omits these, but presents others which seem, and indeed are, contradictory. What is he then to do? The solution is simple: he is to take his club and find out for himself which of the two gives, in his case, the best results, or, in other words, which of the two, after a fair trial, is easiest to him personally. For that is one of the unspeakable benefits of golf: the easiest method of accomplishing the same feat is for each player the right method.

The chapter for parents and guardians, finally, is humbly put forward for those only who are thoroughly mediocre performers, and find they do not improve. It will not, it is hoped, at any rate, do them any harm.

CONTENTS.

LIST OF ILLUSTRATIONS.

PART I.

How to Play Golf

BY

JAMES BRAID
(Open Champion, 1901, &c.)

PART I.

TEE SHOTS.

THERE are five varieties of drive which ought to be within the reach of every first-rate player: he ought at any rate to be able to make a conscious attempt to drive his ball from the tee in such a way as to tend to produce five broad and distinct lines of flight, all with the same object, namely, that the ball may eventually come to rest as far as possible from the tee in the required direction. All minor differences, as, for instance, sparing a ball, in the case of an exceptionally long drive, so that it may not run the risk of going into a bunker which is possibly within the limits of the best, or such natural accidents as an exceptionally high bank or bunker-face so near the tee that there is a risk of a normally driven ball not clearing it, will be left out of the question.

The five main varieties of drive then are as follows :—

(i.) The ordinary full shot.

(ii.) A ball driven high, so as to secure an intentionally long carry, without regard to subsequent run.

(iii.) A ball driven intentionally low, so as to secure exceptionally long run.

(iv.) A ball driven with intentional pull to use or neutralize certain conditions of wind.

(v.) A ball driven with intentional slice, to use or neutralize certain conditions of wind.

These I will take in turn.

(i.) *The ordinary full shot.*—Stance and

grip must necessarily vary a good deal with individual players. My own stance is given in the following diagram.

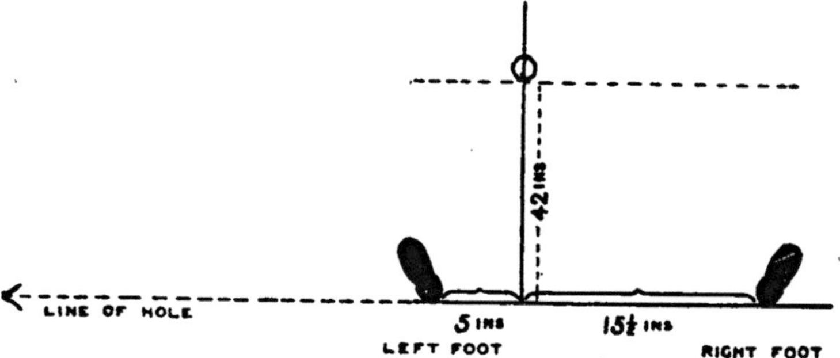

The ball, that is to say, lies at a distance of forty-two inches from the line between my heels, which are twenty and a half inches apart. It is five inches to the right of my left heel. The toes are both considerably turned out, so as to include an angle of about sixty-five degrees.

My own grip is as follows :—

Left hand.—The fork of first finger and thumb of the left hand I place slightly over to the right of the centre of the shaft, the thumb lying directly down the right side of the shaft. I grip the club entirely with my fingers, which throughout the stroke I hold as far as possible rigid.

Right hand.—Here also I grip with my fingers. The little finger lies on the top of the forefinger of my left hand; the two next fingers grip the club, and the forefinger holds it in the crook of its middle joint, while the right thumb rests to the left of the centre of the shaft The whole position of the right hand can be indicated by the fact that the left thumb (held in the manner described) lies in the centre of the palm of the right hand. With the right hand I grip fairly tight. It will be seen from this that I hold my hands very close together; this, I think, makes it easier for them to act in unison.

Stance and grip together will give the

reader an accurate idea of my whole position, when I have addressed the ball and am completely ready to swing. As there is a good deal of difficulty about getting a satisfactory photograph of any player absolutely at the top of his swing, owing to the short time the club is at rest there, it may be of interest to describe what I believe to be the position of the arms, the club-head, and the wrists at this moment. Of the action of the wrists—a most important piece of mechanism to work properly into the swing — I shall speak at length later.

At this moment (*i.e.*, the moment when the club and arms are both motionless between the upward and downward swings), the left arm is slightly bent upwards from the elbow, the elbow being about opposite the centre of the chest, the right arm similarly is bent upwards from the elbow, the elbow being about six inches away from the body and twelve inches below level of right shoulder. Both wrists must be underneath the club, the head of which should be a shade higher than the hands and the face, and the toe of the club should be pointing directly downwards. The grip of the hands should be easy, but not loose.

I hope I shall be excused for speaking somewhat fully about the part that the wrists play in the drive, since I attribute the length of my own drive to the fact that I have very powerful wrists, and use them to the utmost at the moment of hitting full shots. "Putting the wrists into it" is a very common phrase, but to do this successfully is difficult of accomplishment, and in a way difficult to understand. But what I believe to be my method is as follows:—

The wrists are "put into it" with a quick forward movement just before the club-head meets the ball. It is this forward movement, a click as it were, on the top of the swing of the arms, that gives the ball the extra impetus. The difficulty does not lie in this last movement, but in the part the wrists have previously taken in the stroke. Beginning then from the beginning, after the ball has been addressed, the first movement of the left wrist (which is the important one, it guiding, the right following) is to turn the left hand inwards from the wrist, till, when the club is about half-way up on the upward swing, the back of the left hand is level, *i.e.*, horizontal with the ground. From that point, still by a gradual motion, following the swing of the club the left hand is further brought round by the wrist till at the top of the swing it is bent back to be perpendicular to the ground. This process has to be gone through without force, since the use of force throws the player out of position. Still without force, on the part of wrists, the downward swing is performed (with the movement of the wrists of course reversed) until the club-head is about fifteen inches from the ball. At that point the wrists should be fairly rigid, and in the same position as that in which they left the ball on the upward swing. But from that point—and here comes in the work they play in the stroke—they should be given a sharp forward movement with their full force. It is this that gives the ball its impetus. It must be borne in mind, of course, that though the different parts of the stroke are here described, all these processes form the one swing; indeed it is exactly the "jerky" element which so often spoils the stroke.

In this "putting the wrists into it" the mistake most players fall into is in lifting the club for the upward swing without immediately beginning to turn the wrists as described; instead they *pull* away the club with the wrists rigid, thus, as a consequence, using the right hand too much, which ought to follow the left, and not allowing the head of the club to go first, as it should do.

So much then for the normal drive, that is to say, on a calm day when there is no wind, or at any rate not wind enough to make a new factor.

(ii.) *A ball driven with an intentionally long carry.*—This drive is useful when there is a strong wind behind, or possibly when the ground is exceedingly wet and dead, so that a ball has practically no run in any case; or again when, in combination with a wind behind, it will certainly pitch on a steep slope against it, so that again there will be no run.

But in the main a high ball is useful in a strong following wind, since the longer it remains in the air, the longer it will reap benefit from the wind. In this case it is simply necessary to play the ball as before described, using a higher tee. With the wind behind I generally use a tee three-quarters of an inch high.

(iii.) *A ball driven intentionally low.*— This drive is obviously useful when there is a strong wind against the player, since a high ball will necessarily encounter the wind more than a low one, and, if not actually taken back, at any rate will be so killed in the air that it will not run when it pitches. Thus the energy employed in getting the ball high will obviously be better used in making it keep low. Also a low ball will always run more than a high one.

Here, conversely to playing with a following wind, it is advisable to use as low a tee as possible, about a quarter of an inch, while the right wrist should be slightly turned over at the moment of striking the ball.

(iv.) *A ball driven with intentional pull.*—This may be useful in several ways: if, for instance, there is a dangerous bunker at limit of carry in straight line a ball played to the right with pull will frequently go round and beyond it. But the stroke is most useful (as a tee shot) when there is a strong wind from the right, and a long ball is wanted. Now it might occur to some reader that if the wind is from the right, a ball should be played with a slight slice, so as to neutralize the tendency of the wind to carry it to the left. That is quite true, but a ball so driven will never be a long one, since very soon after it has left the tee, as soon, in fact, as the slice begins to tell, it will be fighting the wind all the way, will lose impetus very quickly, and eventually drop dead. Instead, the proper course is to play into the wind, *i.e.*, to the right of the hole, with a slight pull on it.

Thus as soon as the pull begins to tell, the ball will be helped all the way by the wind, and when it pitches, instead of pitching dead, will run.

For an intentionally pulled ball, I grip in the ordinary manner, but the stance, both with regard to the position of the ball to the feet, and the feet to the line of the hole, is different. Instead of teeing the ball as described in the diagram five inches behind heel of left foot and twenty in front of heel of right, I stand with the ball half-way between the two feet. Again, instead of the line through the feet being in direction of hole, I stand with right foot drawn about four inches back. Also at the moment of striking the ball, the head of the club must not be on the same perpendicular as the ball and the hands, but in front of the hands. Finally (this will be found to be a natural consequence from the alteration of the stance), the toe of the club must be slightly turned in at the moment of striking the ball.

(v.) *A ball intentionally sliced.* — This stroke is usually employed in the converse of circumstances under which the player should intentionally pull a ball, that is to say, he should play with slice into the wind when the wind is from the left.

In order to secure this I grip in the usual manner, but stand a little more behind the ball, so that it is nearly on a level with the heel of my left foot, and, as in intentional pulling I draw the right foot back, so in intentional slicing I advance it about six inches, so that the stance is more open, while the left toe is pointing nearly directly to the hole. In playing the stroke I drop the right shoulder a little, turn out the heel of the club, and get the hands in front of the head of the club at the moment of hitting. The stroke indeed varies from the normal in exactly the opposite manner as that described for getting pull.

With regard to the clubs themselves I personally play with clubs that are light in comparison to my strength, and short in comparison to my height. With a short light club in the hands one has more complete control over its movements than with a heavy one, and in consequence there is a gain in point of accuracy, since a heavy club is apt to "run away with one." Nor do I believe that a heavy club gives a longer ball. The shaft should have a little spring in it, just enough in fact to make the club feel easy. But if the shaft is very whippy, owing to some personal preference, the player should always swing very quietly, since the whippiness puts an increased difficulty in timing the stroke. For with a very whippy shaft, if a violent quick swing is taken, the hands and grip of the club are on the perpendicular above the ball before the head. On the other hand, if a shaft is perfectly rigid it is necessary to force the stroke—thus risking accuracy in order to get a long ball.

With regard to material I find persimmon is rather brittle, and liable to split, but dog-wood, of the newer woods, is almost unbreakable and very good in wet weather, as rain does not seem to soften the face of it. But neither of these give such a nice "feel" as the beechwood club, nor, in my own opinion, do they get such a long ball. I always prefer a wooden-faced club, but if the club must be faced, good leather (only the leather must be good) comes nearest to wood. Fibre-facing I do not like at all, though it is hard to say why. The ball does not seem to go off it "sweet," nor is there sufficient spring in it.

Finally, in the case of any player beginning golf after the age of thirty or so, I should recommend him to cultivate a short swing rather than attempt a full one. He is far more likely to be accurate with a short swing, for unless a full swing has grown up with you, it is not likely to be very reliable. For such a player I should recommend a short and rather heavy club, as from the nature of the swing he must be giving more of a blow to the ball than a man with the natural free full swing.

PLAY THROUGH THE GREEN.

From the moment the ball is struck from the tee, a great many additional complications come into the game; it gets harder and harder till the hole is reached. On the tee you can place the ball and stand where you like, but through the green you have to play the ball where it lies and stand where you can.

In the fairway of a course, leaving out of the question for a moment anything like bunkers, cups and hollows or bent, there are four main divergencies for the tee shot in the way a ball may lie. Thus it may lie well enough in itself, *i.e.*, it may lie cleanly, but it may lie—

(i.) Above where the player must stand.

(ii.) Below where the player must stand.

(iii.) With a slope upwards in direction of hole.

(iv.) With a slope downwards in direction of the hole, giving what is commonly called a hanging ball.

All these four, to be properly and satisfactorily played, so that the ball may go cleanly in the required direction, necessitate, as is natural, a certain alteration in stand and grip, in order to allow for the variations in position from the lie of a ball on a level tee.

(i.) When the ball is lying above where the player must stand.

Here the grip of a club must be shortened in order to allow for the height of the ball above the feet. The player will also find that he gets more into his natural position with regard to the ball if he leans a little forward, so as to bring his hands more directly over it. The swing must be easy, and it is important to remember that the best played ball from this position will have a slight pull on it, which should be allowed for. The pull perhaps is due to the natural and proper instinct of the player to turn in the toe of the club a little so as to keep the heel from striking the ground.

(ii.) When the ball lies below where the player must stand.

Here the opposite tactics hold good. The

club must be gripped at its fullest length, in order to counterbalance the distance the ball is below the stance of the feet, and the weight must be put well on to the heels, in order to avoid the tendency, due to the slope of the ground, to fall forward over the ball. There is also a tendency to slice a ball in this position, and a slight slice should be allowed for.

(iii.) When the ball lies on a slope upwards in direction of the hole.

Here the right shoulder must be dropped a little, for this reason, that if the ball was played with level shoulders, the club could not follow through properly, but would strike the opposing slope and be checked. The player should intentionally consider this follow through, and with the same object in view keep the weight of his body well on the right heel, which, in conjunction with the dropping of the right shoulder, will put him, so to speak, on the same plane as the ball, which he can then play in his ordinary manner.

(iv.) When the ball is lying on a slope downward, in direction of a hole.

This ball, commonly called a hanging-ball, is responsible for more mis-hits than probably any other, and many first-class players never feel comfortable over it. This is partly due to the fact that most players will play at the ball as if it was lying flat, and also because most players, from experience, are instinctively afraid of it, and from nervousness make a bad shot, usually a topped one. In this shot it is best to stand a little more than usual behind the ball, so as to give it a certain amount of cut which will make the ball rise more quickly, since it is of primary importance to get it well away from the ground. Keep the weight of the body, as in No. iii., well on the right foot, and look (for once) not at the ball, but at the ground immediately behind it, and play the stroke, not with the looseness natural to an ordinary shot, but more firmly. All these precautions are devoted to the one end of getting the ball well and quickly off the ground, and for the same reason I should never use a straight-faced driver, but a slightly lifted club.

Now, though it is often desirable to put slice or pull on to a ball, it is much oftener desirable not to, and it is most important to be able if possible as soon as the fault occurs to correct a tendency to do either of these, and keep the ball straight.

When a player finds he has a tendency to slice, I should suggest the following as a corrective, which, it will be seen, is partly the same as I recommend for an intentional pull off the tee. Thus the right foot should be a little drawn back, and care should be taken that the club-head should be carried through in front of the body, not pulled by the arms after the rest of the club. Another common cause of slicing arises from not playing straight at the ball, but bringing the club-head across it. This is due to the fault of not letting the arms go free through, but pulling them in during the downward part of the swing. Often also a player can correct this tendency by attending carefully to his follow through, for provided the follow through be full and correct, the tendency to slice will probably vanish, for the simple reason that the club must have hit the ball correctly. This, in any case, in conjunction with the drawing back of the right foot, supposing the fault lies in the stance, will go a long way to correct slicing.

Conversely, if the player finds he has a tendency to pull, he should advance the right foot a little, standing at the same time a trifle more behind the ball, and as in correcting slicing it is important to get the club-head carried through well in front of the body, so in pulling he will find it useful to get the body into the stroke a little quicker, though without any jerk. At the same time he should turn the heel of the club out a little, so that the head should meet the ball squarely, not with the toe pointing upwards.

But perhaps of all faults possible through the green the commonest and most expensive is topping. In order to correct this (but not afterwards when it has been remedied), though "keep your eye on the ball" is one of the first maxims of golf, I recommend the player to keep his eye not on the ball but on the ground immediately behind it. The reason for this is that he has been looking probably at the top of the ball (a sufficient reason for hitting it there), and a conscious effort to look behind it will probably result in his looking at the right place. In addition, in playing the stroke he should keep the weight of the body largely on the right foot, and get his right shoulder more down. All these correctives, it will be noticed, hang together, they all aim at the same thing in fact, *i.e.*, getting the club-head more surely behind at the moment of striking. Care should also be taken to keep the body, and particularly the head, steady and not to lift the club up too quickly in the upward swing. Finally the eye should not be lifted too soon in the follow through, since it is easily possible that looking up before the ball has been fairly struck has been responsible for the topping, and conscious intention to continue looking at the place where the ball has been, after it is gone, will very likely remedy this.

One of the most difficult ties a player will encounter through the green, is a cuppy tie, where the ball lies cleanly enough, it may be, but with higher ground both immediately behind and in front of it. Here two special provisions must be made to get the ball cleanly away, for the club must be brought down not in its ordinary manner, or else it would catch the lip of ground behind the ball, and it must also lift the ball more quickly than usual, or the ball itself will in the first moment of its flight hit the ground in front. The club therefore should in the upward swing be lifted more upright, and brought down more upright, so as to nip in between the ball and the rise behind it. Also, as in a hanging lie, the player should try to get on a little cut, so that the ball may rise more quickly. The body must be kept more steady and not allowed to be loose as in the ordinary shot, and the hands should grip more firmly than usual.

In such a lie as this, and indeed in all lies through the green unless the ball is lying exceptionally well, I use, if a wooden club at all, not a driver but a brassy. And even if the ball is lying unusually well, I use a driver with a slight loft instead of a straight-faced driver, the reason being that the ball is on the ground, not, as when on the tee, on an artificially raised spot, which naturally gives it the loft desirable.

With regard to full shots with the cleek or driving iron, the swing should be exactly the same as with a driver, except that it is a shade more upright. As opposed to driver shafts, the shaft of all iron clubs should, in my opinion, be always stiff, and never whippy. These with driver and brassy are the only clubs with which I take a completely full swing, since with lofted clubs there is a universal tendency to pull a full shot. Then with an iron I never go quite so far back as with a play club, and with a mashie I never attempt a full swing. In fact until I am well within their carrying distance I do not use them at all.

It has been seen that with a certain object, *i.e.*, that of raising the ball more quickly than its natural flight would allow, cut must be put on a ball, but it never should be put on unless it is absolutely necessary, as in such cases as I have spoken of, or when a ball must be pitched on to a green, because it is closely guarded by a bunker or bad ground, and would without cut infallibly roll off it again. It is very difficult to judge both how much cut is necessary, and how much one is putting on, but cut may be used with some degree of accuracy up to about 120 yards, for purposes of checking the run of a ball. But unless it is necessary, unless there is no easier way of getting near the hole, I never put it on.

Thus, to take a concrete example, if the ball is lying 60 yards, let us say, from the near edge of a green, and 80 yards from the hole itself, a player should not attempt to pitch it fairly on to the green, but pitch a low shot with the mashie, somewhere about the edge of the green, and let the ball's natural run take it across the whole width of the green. Or again at a greater distance where the mashie will not carry I should very often use an iron, and intentionally hit a low shot with the object of pitching considerably short, and running up on to the green. For this shot it is necessary to stand slightly more in front of the ball than usual, and at the moment of hitting turn the club over a little with the right hand.

Sometimes it is absolutely necessary in

order to save the hole to play a full shot from a thoroughly bad lie out of thick grass or heather, where one would have naturally played a safe shot, get out, that is to say, without going much distance, and hope for a better lie. Here there is a great danger in the first place of the club-head as it encounters the heather or thick grass of turning and thus not hitting the ball fairly. So the player should first of all hold the club very tightly in order to prevent this. He should also place his feet as firmly as possible, for he will have to play not an ordinary full shot but a forcing shot, and it is imperative that he should be quite firm, or he will mis-hit. For this reason also he should use the body as little as possible, and not attempt at all to use his wrist, which should remain quite rigid when the ball is struck.

It will be remembered that from the

tee, if there is a strong wind from the right, I recommended a ball played with slight pull into the wind with a view to getting the assistance of the wind, and conversely with a wind from the left, a ball played with a little slice. But when the green is within easy distance of the club the player is going to use, I recommend exactly the opposite tactics, and playing rather harder than I should if there was no wind, I should put a little slice on to a ball if the wind is from the right for these reasons. The ball will fly into the wind, fighting it, and lose its initial force while in the air. It will thus when it falls, fall perpendicularly, and thus very dead, without any run in it. Also the slice counterbalanced by the push of the wind will take it eventually straight. In the same way with a wind from the left I would try to play with a slight pull. These shots, however, must not be considered easy; they have to be very well timed, and the player must be able to estimate the amount of pull or slice necessary. Such shots also are useful where there is some reason (an intervening bunker for instance) for pitching on the green and not running.

It remains to consider (after this examination of lies on the fair way of the course) the best way of setting to work when bunkered. In far the majority of cases, as when the ball is in a ditch, a rut, or with a bunker face in front, it is much wiser to take a niblick and be content merely to get out. But occasionally in a bunker there is an opportunity to get a long shot, and that is when the ball is lying cleanly (not in a depression or heel mark), on level sand, and when there is no bunker face in front. In these cases I very often take a brassy or cleek, though I do not play the ordinary full shot. It is important first of all not to move the feet at all, since any movement or turn on them will probably make one or the other sink into the sand and thus alter the stance while the stroke is being played. This of course would be fatal in such a lie, since the very least inaccuracy will cause the player either to top the ball or to take too much sand before he hits it, which is equally fatal. The average player nearly always moves about on his feet too much, thus altering their position, and he also swings the body too much. An additional difficulty of course is the fact that he is not allowed to ground the club when addressing ball. I should recommend him therefore to keep the feet still, not lifting the heel at all in the upswing, to keep his head and body particularly steady, and play with the arms only, thus making the stroke far more of a hit than the ordinary swing. He will not get of course full distance out of the stroke, but he has a reasonable chance if he will stand steady and play with the arms, of getting a distance which would have been utterly impossible with a niblick or a lofted club.

But in the majority of bunker lies, ditches, wheel ruts, &c., the niblick must be used. This club must always be gripped very tightly, as it has to get through obstacles before it reaches the ball. It must be swung rather upright and with the arms only, while the feet should not be moved, but placed as firmly as possible wherever the stance is. If the ball is lying in a depression in sand, the stroke must be aimed not at the ball at all, but at the sand some inch or so behind it, since the ball has, so to speak, to be dug out. So also the club must be brought up sharply after hitting the ball, not allowed to follow through in the ordinary manner, since thus it will have the effect of making the ball rise more sharply.

THE PUTTING GREEN.

It is sometimes said that there is no use in practising putting, since it gives you only familiarity with the green you are practising on. I do not agree with this, since it is only by practice that the eye can be trained and kept trained to judge distance and the lie of the ground.

When it comes to the actual putting, if there is any question about the line, I look at the putt from behind the ball and secondly from the other side of the hole. If the lines seem to differ, I choose the line which appears right from the other side of the hole.

In all putts, long or short, I do not play

with the wrist or forearm merely, but with the whole arm, and never tap or hit the ball, but follow through. In all putts the player should stand firm and not move the body at all. In addressing the ball it is well to take a little time, but not too long, as a putt never gets easier by looking at it.

The short putt—*i.e.*, of five feet or under—the player should always play sufficiently hard to go about six inches past the hole if he misses it, for in these short putts many holes are lost by the ball stopping short of the hole. Other common causes of missing them when the ball appears absolutely dead, are that the player does not take his club straight back, thus putting slice or pull on the ball, also that he often looks at the hole too soon when he should be still looking at the ball. Moving the body is another common cause of missing short putts.

There are many excellent putters who putt in apparently very different manners, but I think it will be found that they all have certain points in common, namely :—

(i.) They all try to putt over some object (blades of grass, &c.) lying between them and the hole, but nearer to the ball than the hole.

(ii.) They all try to lay a long putt dead, but on the far side of the hole.

(iii.) They all keep their heads and bodies perfectly steady.

With regard to the question of stymies, about which many players all disagree, I should vote for their abolition, except in such cases where the player has laid himself one.

In playing them, should they arise, confidence is necessary. The mashie should be used and must be gripped very tight. The ball should be lofted with a slight cut, the wrists only to be used. The hardest of all stymies is when the opponent's ball is quite close to the hole, and the ball has to be pitched definitely into the hole. When, however, the opponent's ball is nine inches or farther away, the ball should be pitched between the other and the hole, and allowed to run.

PART II.

How to Play Golf

BY

J. A. T. BRAMSTON

Preliminary Position for Drive.

[*To face page* 43.

PART II.

CHAPTER I.

THE game of golf begins with a paradox. The wail of the beginner is always the same —"If only I could drive." And in this he undoubtedly finds the most difficulty. The reason for this, however, is merely lack of knowledge, or perhaps experience. He has not yet discovered the devilish ingenuity with which the ball will sit on the edge of the hole, or the predilection which it seems to have for pitching against the side of a mound, after it has been well struck with an approaching club, and then rolling slily into a neighbouring bunker.

Golf becomes increasingly difficult in proportion as one gets nearer to the green, and once arrived there many people will give it as their opinion that the real test of skill begins. But be that as it may, in championship matches quite seven-tenths of the holes are won simply and solely on the green, owing to one of the players taking three or more putts, or more rarely by a long steal or a very accurate pitch, which enables the fortunate competitor to get "down" in one as against the more orthodox two of his partner. These facts, however, are as yet outside the experience of the tyro, and he feels that life would be really worth living, provided only that he could hit the ball hard and high with his driver.

But if the question of driving is examined at all carefully, it must be obvious that, theoretically, at any rate, it is by far the easiest part of the game.

The ball is placed in what the player considers the most suitable position on the tee, and it then has to be struck, not any definite distance, but as far as possible in the direction of the hole.

The difficulty of calculating the required strength does not come in at all to complicate the stroke, and, moreover, if we except the exigencies of the wind, the drive is purely mechanical, or, in other words, all drives are exactly alike, the object being in every case to get as far from the tee and as near to the hole as possible.

No doubt there are a great many practical difficulties at first to be encountered in learning how to drive, but when once a man, or, better still, a boy, has acquired a swing and has satisfied himself that it is the best that he has in him, it becomes a real possession, and the driving difficulty at any rate does not recur.

As for the present writer, though he has found that the methods he recommends have given respectable results, he is yet perfectly aware that different methods have given and will give results not inferior; as these, however, are not his own, he cannot speak of them with any authority. Still, to the "introspective golfer," certain points seem to be common to players, whose styles are widely different. Sound exponents of the game, whether from design or unconscious imitation, have adapted to their own requirements certain peculiarities which give the soundest results. Obviously, then, these are the points worth learning, or, in other words, they are the essentials, the real picture, of which the rest of the style is merely the frame. The frame is unimportant, being absolutely arbitrary. Each player has his own idiosyncrasies. He adopts from his own experience the style which comes easiest to him. But these common points can be acquired equally well from the pages of a book and from the *vivâ voce* teaching of a professional.

The photographs have, whenever practicable, been taken from behind, and it is hoped that such readers as have felt the difficulty of getting into the positions indicated by frontal pictures will find this means of illustration more easy to follow, should they consider it worth their while.

CHAPTER II.

AT THE BEGINNING OF THE SWING.

Of the Stance.—Stance is absolutely immaterial. It is only necessary to glance at some of the leading golfers to perceive the infinite variety of stances which can be used with success. At one extreme there is Mr. J. E. Laidlay, who stands with the ball exactly opposite, if not actually outside, the left foot. At the other is J. H. Taylor, with the ball facing the right foot. The intervening spots between these two extreme points, on which the ball can be placed, are all occupied by good players, nor can it be said that any one is preeminently better than the rest. What each player has to aim at is a reasonable position from which he feels most competent to hit the ball at the right elevation, and this he can find out best for himself by experiment.

A practical hint, however, may be given to the beginner.

Let him imagine the space between his feet divided into three equal sections by the two lines AB and CD as follows :—

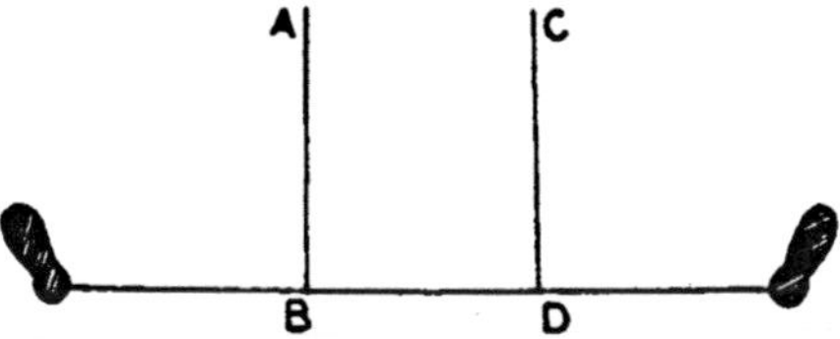

Then if he chooses to drive more off the left foot than the right, he will find that the most comfortable position will be obtained by putting the ball at the point A. This gives a perfectly normal stance, without any exaggeration or eccentricity. If, however, he prefers to play more off the right foot, the ball goes naturally to the point C. This is perhaps a slightly more constrained position, and does not in the beginner conduce quite so much to straightness as the former.

But it is a good working stance, and one to be considered when learning the game. The great point to be urged in favour of getting the ball well forward is that, as the club-head is just getting to the ball, it is just beginning to rise, so that the upward tendency is imparted to the ball, at the same time, and the accomplishing of this, as has been said, is an almost insurmountable obstacle to a man when he first takes up golf.

In spite of the unimportance of the stance, there is one thing almost, if not quite, essential to produce a habit of creditable shots. This is to be comfortable. Again and again a man is to be seen obviously ill at ease after he has taken up his position. He shifts his feet, turns the club in and out, glances up at the hole, and in a word evinces a lively dissatisfaction with his present surroundings. This invariably is a prelude to missing the shot, and the cause was that he was uncomfortable when he made it. And yet few have a sufficiency of common-sense to begin all over again ; to stand quite clear of the ball, and then come up to it to address it anew. The majority are content with slight alterations in the placing of their feet, which in all probability carry them further and further away from the comfort, which is almost synonymous with success. For if a player feels comfortable on addressing the ball, he has successfully accomplished the first stage in his journey towards the hole.

Don't be satisfied with makeshifts, but start again. For the best position is the most natural one, and that must be attained naturally and not by the shuffling of shoes, or, worse still, by mathematical measurements.

Having established the feet and the ball in a satisfactory position, an enquiry must be held into the other component parts, which make up the whole preliminary action.

Of the knees.—In the first place, almost all players keep the knees bent when addressing the ball, and certainly all players who aim at a "flat" swing. The whole question is one of balance. Let a man take a club and stand with his knees stiff. He will find that in order to get the club into its proper position behind the ball, he will have to bend his body forward from the hips, so that it is shaped like a C, with the result that all the weight of the body is thrown upon the front part of the feet, and he is only slightly removed from being on tiptoe. Then let him swing the club up and down, exerting the same force as would be used in an actual stroke, and he will find that he has lost his balance, and will have to step forward, in order to save himself from tumbling on his face. But if the knees are bent, and more especially the left one, for reasons which will be dealt with later, the back is naturally in a straight line and not curved into an obnoxious C-shape, and the player will feel that the weight of his body is almost entirely on the heels, with the result that he feels himself more secure, and more competent to retain his feet in their original position at the end of the swing.

Of the heels.—While upon this subject, it may be worth while to mention a test by which one can form an opinion of a man's driving powers without seeing the actual stroke, provided that he has left the marks of his feet upon the tee. If, after striking the ball, the player's heels are in the same spot as when he originally took up his stance preliminary to playing, he can be catalogued as a straight and consistent, if not a very long, driver. Any movement of his heels marks him at once as a more or less erratic and uncertain hitter. This is a necessary fact. For movement of the two bases upon which ultimately the whole body is sustained, must imply loss of balance, and consequent loss of accuracy in hitting the ball. It cannot be too strongly urged that the heels are the proper weight-supporters in the various shots at golf, and by bending the knees the weight is thrown instantly upon the heels, so that a firm base is obtained for the whole body.

The second essential, then, is this, to keep the weight well back on the heels. The natural tendency of all beginners is to fall over forwards, and it is only by grasping this essential point that they will be able to counteract this fault, and, by getting their balance, to attain to consistency in all the shots.

Of the club-head.—The next subject for consideration is the position of the club-head when at rest behind the ball. There are two points to be guarded against, one absolutely and the other partially.

The absolute fault is to turn in the nose of the club so as to counteract a slice. This implies the most heinous crimes in the rest of the stroke, and is a mere makeshift attempt to produce a satisfactory result by unsatisfactory means without going down to the root of the fault, which in all probability lies, as will be shown later, in the right shoulder or right knee. The other is a more venial point, but still one of which it is advisable to steer clear, namely,the practice of putting the club-head down with the toe opposite to the near edge of the ball. This, in any but a seasoned golfer, who may claim to know his own mind upon such matters, implies a tendency to fall in upon the ball; or, in other words, shows that the player has not got his balance perfectly, and consequently he has to allow for the lurch forward, which he knows, though perhaps only sub-consciously, will come at the moment when he is putting out his strength to the full. But this extra calculation adds very largely to the difficulty of the stroke, and of course militates against both accuracy and consistency. In fact both these faults arise from a concession to weakness, from a desire to use the hoe and not the spade in eradicating blemishes. They should not come even into the ken of a self-respecting golfer. In this matter, as in almost all others in the game, the natural position is the least open to objection, with certain exceptions when mere straightness is not aimed at. Let the club-head rest easily upon the ground, in such a way that the centre of the ball is opposite the exact spot upon the club face, with which it is afterwards to be struck. This is the straightforward and, it might almost be said, honourable thing to do. It rather suggests showing a horse an obstacle before putting him at it, so as to give him some idea of what is expected from him. It may be noticed that no censure has been applied to the trick of turning the club face slightly up or out. The reason is that it really does not matter to any appreciable extent. Many clubs are built with a tendency in this direction and there is something to be said for it. For it certainly encourages the ball to fly well up into the air, and there is no serious danger of a slice provided that the right knee and shoulder do their work properly.

Of the methods of addressing the ball.—In the methods of addressing the ball, there are two distinct characteristics to be found in the two great golfing nations.

Mr. J. L. Low, in writing of the inter-varsity matches of the last few years, has applied the terms "restive," "boisterous," "almost rhetorical," to Mr. Norman Hunter's preliminary waggle, and this description brings out well the distinctive character of the Scottish method of address. Mr. Low's antithesis to this rhetorical flourish is described as "whispering to the ball," that is to say, he characterizes the preparations of the average Englishman as more sober and sedate than that of his Northern brother. This classification cannot of course be pressed home in every case, but the method of address affords a strong clue to the nationality of a player, or, at any rate, to the nationality of his golf. One notable reversal of this distinction seems to cry out for recognition, namely, Mr. Horace Hutchinson's somewhat nervous Scottish waggle, as compared with Mr. Leslie Balfour's out-Englishing of the English in the deliberateness of his preparatory movements. The mere fact that such an exception is striking goes a long way to prove the endemic nature of these two varieties of address. But which is best ? The Englishman, if moved to consider the matter, would probably give as the reason for his sedateness, that he was afraid of disturbing his equilibrium before the crucial moment of the stroke. The Scotchman, on the other hand, when provided with his thinking-cap, would probably assert the necessity of a certain amount of preliminary bustle in order to screw himself up to the highest tension before delivering the blow. Unbridled energy does, no doubt, introduce the danger of loss of balance, and also acts as an encouragement to "pressing"; but, on the other hand, it may be that a quiet method of aiming detracts from the length of drive. In any case there is one point of importance common to both types, and that is the necessity of keeping the whole of the body as still as possible, and of allowing the arms and wrists to do all the waggling.

One remark, however, must be made upon a certain most obnoxious style of addressing the ball, and one, moreover, which has "Bad Golfer" writ large all over it. It is, of course, the practice of raising the club slowly up above the shoulder and then bringing it slowly down again to a position of rest behind the ball. It is not only on behalf of the outraged spectators, whose hearts grow sick with deferred hope, that this protest is being made, but also in the interests of the luckless perpetrator of the stroke. The manœuvre described above is always performed with the feet firmly planted on the ground. No shifting of weight takes place. The arms are the sole agents. The result is that, when the club finally goes up for the last time, the stroke, instead of being a graceful flowing motion, degenerates into a mere ungainly flick of wrists and forearm. No use is made of any particle of the rest of the body, and the ball goes, perhaps, a hundred and ten yards. Surely an inadequate distance.

Of the grip.—A good grip of the club implies a good grip of the game. The truth of this statement is abundantly proved by its opposite. Supposing a club to be put into the hands of one of the uninitiated, his method, merely of holding it, betrays him immediately. He invariably grasps it firmly in the palms of his hands as though it were a battle axe. Usually the right hand is held five or six inches lower down the leather than the left; the fingers all look too big for the job which they have to do, for of course there is no room for them on the thin grip, owing to the intrusion of the rest of the hand. Finally, when it comes to the stroke, the wrists are so cramped and impeded by this palm grip, that they are not used at all. The attempt to strike the ball becomes a sharp twitch of the right arm, something in the manner of a man with a stiff wrist bowling fast underhand lobs. Such a travesty as this cannot be called a bad golf shot, for the simple reason that there is no golf in it at all. But it will serve as a means of making clear a more desirable grip, by giving an opportunity of pointing out the fundamental mistakes in each of the points enumerated.

In the first place, the fat part of the hand is not the natural and consequently the correct receptacle for the handle of a golf club, in view of the motions to be gone through afterwards. Golf is played largely with the wrists, and, as everyone will acknowledge after trying it for himself, this palm-grip hampers the wrists and checks their free play, unless the club is held very loosely. No doubt there are certain geniuses who have made a successful use of this grip, but a talented eccentric is not a good standard for imitation, and an attempt to mould one's play on such an example almost invariably ends in disaster.

To quote one instance, there is a Northam player at Westward Ho! who holds his left hand below his right and plays a good game withal. Certainly no one can say that he is wrong, in that he finds it easier to adopt this method, but equally certainly, no one would undertake to copy him, in the expectation of improving his game. A golfer with a strain of genius latent in him soon finds it out when he has attained proficiency at the game, but until this peculiarity proclaims itself, he will probably do best to follow the canons which are accepted by ninety out of every hundred of his fellow golfers.

The normal and advisable golfing grip consists in holding the club in the fingers of both hands. Begin by laying the club-head in position on the ground, supported entirely by the little finger of the left hand, which is coiled round the handle like a hook. Then carry on this gripping process with the other fingers in succession, the first finger of the left hand being followed by the little finger of the right. These two fingers must be pressed as closely as possible together to insure homogeneity of movement between the two hands. The first finger of the right hand is best separated a little from its pre-

The Beginning of the Grip

[*To face page* 64

decessor, the second finger, to enable the club to be "felt" by the joints of the first finger. For it is from the crook thus formed that much of the power of the shot and all the "touch" is obtained. The club is then held entirely in the eight fingers and some employment has to be found for the thumbs. These should be brought across the handle, and should close upon the spaces left unoccupied by the tips of the first and second fingers of each hand, so that the thumb-joints are pressed firmly against the leather. The position of the hands then is as follows. The knuckles of all the fingers are in a straight line along the under side of the handle, pointing directly to the ground, and the apex of the angle formed by the junction of the thumb and first finger of each hand is pointing directly to the shoulders, the right to the right shoulder, and the left to the left.

The club thus held is absolutely firm in the hands. The pressure is extended well over the handle, and every finger helps to tighten the grip. If, however, it were grasped in the clenched fist of a pugilist, the thumbs would be mere supernumeraries, and the full holding power would not be exerted. It is particularly noticeable what great pressure is exerted by the two little fingers. Their immense gripping power was suggested to the present writer by a fisherman, whose whole life had been spent in handling ropes and lines. Both of his fourth fingers from constant use at his work had been bent down against the palms of the hands and were fixed in this curious position. But if these fingers play such an important part in fishing, they in all probability are of value to the golfer; and most players, if, after taking their stance to address the ball, they will examine the nail

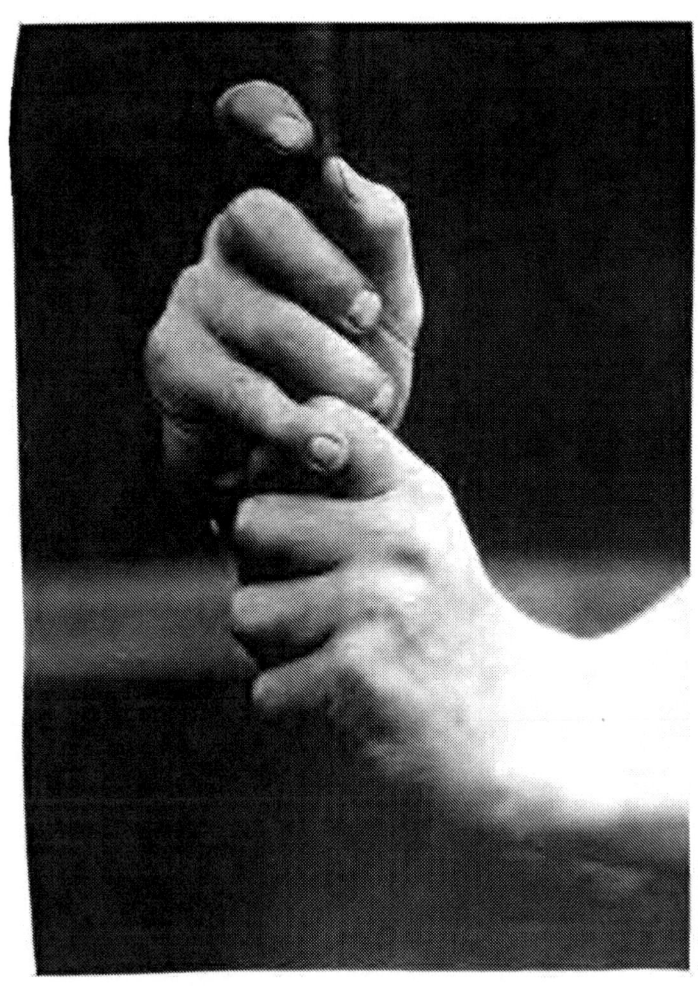

Grip Showing Method of Linking the Fingers.

[*To face page* 66

of the little finger, especially of the right hand, will find a white mark there, indicating that the blood has been momentarily driven away owing to the greatness of the pressure exerted.

The reason seems to be that the little finger of the left hand is the last line of defence by which the club is checked, when it is going forward in the course of the address. The whole question of the grip may seem very complicated, but that is the great difficulty of paper teaching. "Books are good enough in their way, but they are a mighty bloodless substitute for life."

A large number of golfers, realizing the importance of getting the two hands as close together as possible, have adopted the device of separating the first and second fingers of the left hand, so as to form a crook, and then of placing the little finger of the right hand on the knuckle of the former. This indubitably helps to make the two hands work together, so that one does not exert more influence than the other, a common fault, which necessarily causes crooked driving. Further, the grip upon the club is not materially weakened; for the little finger can easily cling on the knuckle prepared for it, and it has the effect of forcing the first finger of the left hand tighter than ever against the club. In fact, it is a grip very much to be recommended. The proof of the pudding is in the eating, and it is phenomenally rare to hear of players who have once adopted this grip discarding it, though the sense of insecurity which it gives at first deters many a man from taking to it.

Of the tightness of the grip.—Perhaps the first point urged upon the incipient golfer, when he takes up a club, is that he must hold it tight with the left hand and loose the right. And yet it is hard to see why this should be so. He will be a bold man who will assert that there are any such distinctions to be made when the club is travelling at its greatest speed, that is to say, just before, at the moment of, and immediately after, meeting the ball. Surely the club must then be held as tightly as possible with both hands, both in order to minimize any chance slipping and to impart the maximum of force to the shot. The grip for certain necessary reasons is relaxed at the top of the swing, the handle being held very loosely in the fingers, but, as the club comes down, the hands instinctively tighten until at the moment of greatest energy the greatest pressure is applied to the handle. This seems to be the natural course of events. As a corrective, however, an easy grip with the right hand in addressing the ball may be of great value to the player, who is pulling or slicing, but even then it is not so much for its own intrinsic merit that it is valuable as because it acts as the lubricant, which sets in order that piece of machinery of the stroke, which by being out of gear, caused the deviation from the straight line.

So much for the preliminaries before the actual shot takes place. The player is standing comfortably, the weight of his body well back on his heels; the knees are bent; the club is held firmly in the fingers of both hands; the club-head is at rest, the striking point being exactly behind the centre of the ball, and above all the eyes are glued unswervingly upon the object, which is to be dispatched as far as possible in the direction of the hole.

The next movements of the player demand a fresh chapter.

CHAPTER III.

THE ACTUAL SWING.

Of Method.—N.B.—It will be convenient in describing the motions which are gone through by the player to make use of the points of the compass as follows :—

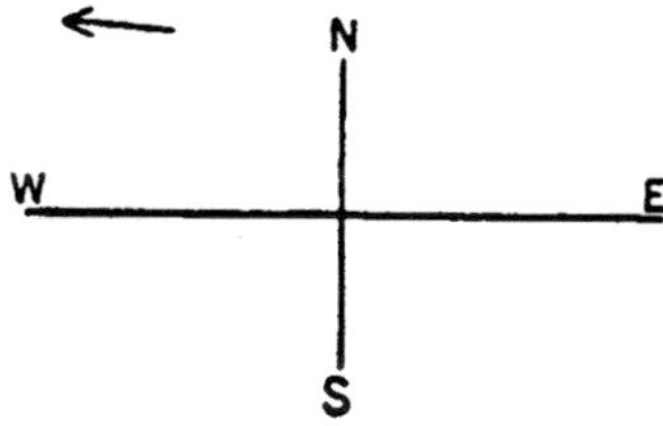

The ball lies to the north, the right and left legs of the player are respectively east and west, and his back is turned towards the south. The direction of the ball is of course from east to west as shown by the arrow head in the diagram.

Of the left leg.—To begin with the lower half of the body, that is the part below the hips—it may be remembered that a recommendation was given to the players to keep both knees bent when addressing the ball, but especially the left. The reason for this is that it has to be both moved and bent in the upward swing, and the movement must be made as easily as possible to prevent loss of balance. For this upward swing is a ticklish business and is apt to upset the equilibrium. What actually happens is that the portion of the weight which was supported by the left leg is shifted across, so that the whole weight of the body rests upon the right. While this fresh disposal of weight is being effected the left knee, which has been facing north-north-

Top of Full Drive.

[*To face page* 72

west, turns to the right, so that at the top of the swing its direction is almost due east. The object then of keeping the left knee well bent is to save the player the difficulty of simultaneously performing the bending of the knee and its turn from west to east at a moment when he has so many other things to think about. As the turn of the knee is completed, the left heel comes off the ground, whatever weight there may be still remaining on the left leg being supported entirely by the toe. This lifting of the heel is apt to be regarded by the novice as a very essential part of the swing, and so to a certain extent it is. But its purpose is not one of cause, but of direct effect. The action of coming up on to the toe is the result of the backward sweep of the club, and can be mentally neglected by the player as it will be performed naturally owing to the position in which he is at the moment. Moreover, the extent to which the heel is raised depends exactly on the length of the backward swing, and players who cannot retain their balance at the top of the swing, owing to the insecurity of the left foot, would do well to shorten their swing to a considerable extent. The toe should retain its original position, pointing north-north-west, and the heel likewise facing about south.

Of the right leg.—As soon as the upward swing begins, the right leg stiffens, owing to the weight of the whole body coming on to it. At this moment, with the exception of the head, it is the only part of the body which is not in motion. Further, it is for the time the pivot on which, together with the circumstance of balance, the whole body depends. Hence it must be as stiff as possible, and the calf and thigh muscles must be quite taut and at their highest tension. Players are recommended to straighten the knee as the club gets to its highest position and to avoid bending it at all at this period of the stroke. If, however, they find it absolutely necessary to bend it, they should do so as little as possible. For naturally a stick with a hinge in it, for instance a folding landing net, is not so reliable a support as a walking stick of the same size and thickness, which is made in one piece only. This ducking of the right knee is very apt to cause a virulent attack of slicing. As the club comes down and the weight of the body is swung on to the left leg, the tension of the right is of course relaxed. At this moment, if the knee is unduly bent, the whole of the right side collapses, the knee becomes incapable of supporting anything and the right shoulder is dropped. Thus a large part of the natural force of the body is abandoned and useless, and the arms instinctively try to supply the lost energy by an extra effort. But owing to the failure of the right shoulder to come through and join in the stroke the hands go forward feebly, while the club-head is left far behind, and when it does ultimately reach the ball, the face is turned right out or north-west, and consequently the shot results in a slice.

One further point to be observed is the necessity of checking the upward flow of the body with the outside of the right foot.

By this means the player can prevent over-swinging himself and so losing his balance.

Of the body.—With regard to the upper part of the body, as the club goes up it turns round on the hips from its original position facing due north, until, at the top of the swing, its direction is due east, exactly opposite that in which the ball is to go. The player should lean slightly away from the ball, to the southward, in order to counteract the tendency to fall forward, which destroys the balance and mars the shot. By so doing he will hollow his back, and this is important. For a rounded back is an abomination in a full shot and bears witness of a very upright swing, of which the off-spring are short, inconsistent and generally unsatisfactory drives. It is noticeable that a very large number of good drivers, in addition to leaning back from the ball, lean also rather in the direction in which the ball is to travel, and so begin to get the body forward even before the top of the swing is reached. This also is an excellent preventative against over-swinging and keeps the player from exerting too much energy before the real business of the downward stroke begins. The result of it is that the club is beginning to travel fast at an early period of the downward swing, and consequently more force is imparted to the ball. There is no dead point of energy when the club has reached its zenith, so that the machinery must needs be started afresh in order to get the club down again. The whole swing works smoothly and without a check.

It is easy to see whether the body is in the right position at the top of the swing by observing the left shoulder. This should be in a direct line north and south between the eyes and the ball, the eyes of course looking over it upon their objective.

The head throughout the whole swing, until the ball has actually sprung away from the club-head, must be held as rigid as is compatible with the necessary give and take. Some players carry the head back during the upward swing so that it faces to the east, but this is extremely inadvisable, for the eye loses sight of the ball altogether and only comes on to it again as the club is descending. Thus an unduly short time is given for proper focussing of the ball, and a topped drive frequently follows. One somewhat extraneous point is worth mentioning in reference to the head, namely, the pipe. It is important for pipe smokers to remember to keep their pipe in the right side of the mouth. Otherwise as the body comes up on to the right leg and the head moves sympathetically an inch or so to the right, a player's pipe bowl intervenes directly between the eye and the ball and most ludicrous results may occur from this temporary cutting off of the vision. Further, a pipe held in the left side of the mouth collides with the left shoulder as it comes into position, and this is apt, if it occurs unexpectedly, to cause a check in the swing and a consequent foozle.

Of the arms.—The two arms have very different parts to play in the upward swing. The left arm should remain almost straight during the whole swing; that is, the angle at the elbow should be very obtuse. This straightness is maintained in the left arm throughout the whole stroke, many players finishing with the club high in the air, in which case it is still stretched out to the full. That, however, for the moment is immaterial. To repeat, in going back the left arm remains practically unbent, and should be carried as far to the east, or even to the south-east, as possible. This keeps the hands at a good distance from the body and makes it difficult for the swing to become cramped. The right arm, however, in opposition to its fellow, begins to bend at the elbow as soon as the club is taken

"'Broken" Finish of Drive.

[*To face page* 80

up. It should be carried well back in a south-easterly direction, and at the top of the swing should be pointing to the ground and immediately to the south. It is most inadvisable to keep the elbow hugged in to the side during this process. A cramped swing is the invariable result. For perfect freedom the elbow should be at least four inches from the right side.

This discussion upon the movements of the arms leads naturally to the wrists and grip. It will be noticed in the photograph opposite that both wrists are dropped. In other words, the hands are bent backwards from the wrists, so that these latter are two or three inches below the handle of the club. This is done in both cases with a definite reason. The left wrist is dropped in order that the hand may be taken as far back as possible, and a freer swing be encouraged. Granted that it is desirable to remove the hands to the greatest possible distance from the body, it will be found that this is most easily effected by dropping the left wrist and loosening the grip of the fingers upon the club handle. Supposing that the original firm grip is maintained and the left wrist is kept in a horizontal position and in the same plane as the shaft of the club, the straightness of the left arm must needs be sacrificed, and the hands brought nearer to the body, which, in the opinion of the present writer, tends to cramp the swing. Further, a discussion was started in *Golf Illustrated* in the year 1900 as to the merits of having the toe of the club pointing directly to the ground at the top of the swing. It was then most strongly upheld that this was the correct position of the club-head, and that its inflexion towards any other point was an attribute of erratic driving. Whether this be so or not, provided that the left wrist is dropped, the club-head does point almost vertically to the ground, whereas, if the wrist is raised and the right grip maintained, the direction of the toe of the club is towards the north.

The object of dropping the right wrist is quite different. It will be found that if it is raised, and, as before, the tight grip maintained, the right elbow must necessarily be raised to the same plane as the club shaft, and sometimes it is even made to point directly to the sky. This position is familiarized to golfers from the fact that it is adopted in every representation of a player engaged in making a full shot, whether it be a model statuette, the engraving upon a medal, or an advertisement of a new waterproof coat. And yet it is surely if not definitely wrong, at least not the most successful style. It affords such great difficulties in keeping on the line.

The arms do not work together at all, but a strong predominance is given to the right, which is, if truth be said, the wrong one. As the club comes down to the ball, if the wrist is bent back, a slice usually occurs, whereas, if it is arched, the result is invariably a hooked shot. The difficulty is that the right arm cannot easily straighten itself from this rather cramped position, and so it comes down bent, and gives the ball a push, without receiving any real assistance from the left arm, to which it should properly be playing only a subordinate part.

To recapitulate the points which have been discussed in the last few pages, it is really important to get the hands well away from the body in an easterly direction, to hold the club loosely in the fingers, in fact, only sufficiently tight to prevent the handle slipping round, and to drop the two wrists. By the first of these manœuvres the club head is encouraged to cling to the ground as long as possible and to come up "flat"; by the last the whole club is prevented from going too far or too high, and is retained in its proper position, namely, level with the player's neck, and to all intents and purposes parallel with the ground. Thus then the player is standing with all his weight on the right leg and foot, wound up like a spring in what he hopes is the best position for uncoiling and launching at the ball.

During the course *of the downward swing*, as the weight of the body comes off the right leg on to the left there is, of course, a moment when it is equally balanced upon the two legs. This is naturally thought to be the moment at which the ball is struck, and one would suppose that a photograph taken *absolutely* instantaneously at the second of striking would give a picture of the player standing equally balanced on both legs, the club-head resting quietly behind the ball. This is almost certainly the view of a vast majority of golfers who have ever given a moment's attention to the point, but with all due respect to such a universal expression of opinion, the present writer begs to maintain a different theory. Surely if a golfer was petrified at the moment of striking, either he would not be in this position, or, if he were, the position of the club-head would infallibly denote a slice, and the more spring there was in the shaft of his club, before it was turned into stone, the greater would be the slice indicated. For even if the club is brought down quite slowly it is found that the club-head is left behind, and that the hands arrive opposite the ball first. How much more then does this happen in a real swing when the club is travelling at its fastest? It is easy to see that at the moment of impinging upon the ball the club-head would be facing outwards and to the right of the proper line of flight. Imagine, then, a man standing equally balanced on both feet, with the face of the club as described. Surely the continuation of such a stroke must result in a bad slice. What really happens, in the opinion of the present writer, is as follows: the weight is already well forward on the left leg and has passed the ball by the time that the club-head reaches it. It has been mentioned that a large number of good drivers lean their bodies at the top of the swing, in the direction in which the ball is to go, and this getting the weight early on to the left leg is only the natural outcome of such a commencement. The body seems to be afraid of being left behind and not coming into the stroke at the right moment. Probably the real reason for this straining forward is to avoid a dead point, when the energy is in course of transition from leg to leg and is absolutely balanced. If the club-head met the ball at this moment, the force of impact could not be the greatest possible. For much, in fact half, of the weight would be still on the right leg, and consequently useless, or even actively detrimental. For it would tend to act as a brake, checking the forward flow of the whole body. But if the weight of the body gets forward, the hands must be left behind to bring along the club, which travels more slowly than the rest of the parts implicated in the stroke. Then at the exact moment of the club reaching the ball, when the wrists and forearms are "creamed up," as they say at Westward Ho! to their fullest tension, and the fingers are gripping their tightest, the hands and club move on into the zone in which the weight of the body is waiting for them, and all three come on to the ball with their full force. In this way there is no real driving off the right leg, although the player may take up his position with the right foot nearer to the ball. All the real driving power comes from the force which is stored on the left leg, and then comes in to the shot when the arms have got down into the position for striking. This being the case, it will be seen that the ball should be struck, not with the exact centre of the club face, but slightly in front of the middle, nearer the toe. For the club comes down with a slight slicing tendency, and this must be corrected.

It is very important as the club comes down to keep the right shoulder as high as possible, in fact level with the left. Any tendency to duck this shoulder is a fatal bar to straightness and length. The balance is lost, since a large part of the weight remains on the right leg, and the ball is hit merely with the arms. Carry the shoulder right through, so that at the end of the swing it is facing due north, towards the spot whence the ball has just been driven.

After the club-head has struck the ball and passed the spot where it lay by six or seven feet, it does not really matter what happens. Of course it cannot be stopped or even checked at once, because the speed at which it has been travelling is terrific, and if a player were able to check the club as soon as it had passed the ball, he would have to have begun to put the brake on before the moment of impact, and so the maximum of force would not have been applied.

As soon as the right wrist has been turned over and the back of this hand is pointing up in the air the stroke is really finished, and the club can be stopped and allowed to fall "brokenly" below the left shoulder. But in order to round off the shot into a thing of real beauty, the arms should be allowed to swing out straight after the ball. The player then is straining forwards towards the hole, and he may be sure that he has "gone through" with his swing even if the ball has been topped.

In the downward swing, as the weight of the body swings off the left leg the heel naturally rises from the ground, using the toe as a pivot, and the leg, with the knee slightly bent, is brought round to face the west. The left leg of course remains absolutely rigid, and this again, as the right in the upward swing, is best not bent at all.

It is important at the end of the swing to maintain the balance by checking the body with the outside of the left foot. Some remarkable positions of the feet are sometimes shown by snapshots. The left heel is often portrayed as the only part of that foot which is on the ground, the toe pointing stiffly up into the air. This, however, is merely an alternative to retain the balance and prevent the body swinging too far. The left foot is forced round by the energy of the swing until it too is facing towards the direction of the hole. Consequently the heel, as a last resource for preventing the body going too far, instinctively is dug into the ground, and, since more pressure can be exerted in this way than when the foot is flat, the toe naturally comes up off the ground.

One word of repetition and we have finished with the driving shot.

Firstly, get the body-weight well forward on to the left leg in the downward swing, and then bring in the wrists as hard as possible, when the club is from four to five feet from the ball. That is the moment

Finish of Drive.

[*To face page* 92

which decides whether the ball is to be a long one, and it is by judicious use of the wrists at that instant that length of drive is to be gained. This is really the much quoted, but seldom understood, " Bring-in-your-wrists."

Secondly, at the moment when the body-weight is brought into the stroke, it must be brought in smoothly and easily. There must be no jerking, but it should do its work like an hydraulic press, quietly, almost unnoticed, and yet irresistibly. Lastly, keep the right shoulder well up, and avoid ducking it, as one would " the venom from a viper," unless the object is to slice the ball.

For such beginners as are trying to acquire a swing, the best advice that can be given is to first acquire their balance. Let the novice take a club and swing it backwards and forwards easily and smoothly without putting the full power into the shot.

He will find that he cannot do this more than three times at the most without shifting his feet to avoid falling on his face. But when he finds himself able to carry out this exercise a dozen or twenty times without loss of balance, he will have won for himself a swing. He will feel the weight shifting from leg to leg, the grip loosening at the top of the swing, and all the parts of the body working harmoniously together. In a word, he will have learnt how to drive.

CHAPTER IV.

Play through the green.—Whenever possible, subject of course to limitations of distance, use a wooden club. In beginners it is only too common a fault to find them discarding their drivers as soon as the ball has been struck from the tee, and ploughing laboriously along the length of the hole with a cleek or iron. This is not the right way to learn to play at golf, much less to play it. The full shot through the green is as much an integral part of the game as the drive from the tee, and it is very often more important, especially on well laid-out courses like St. Andrew's, where so much depends upon the second shot. A full shot on to the green gives the finest sensation of any stroke in the game, and many a novice would be spurred on to a higher golfing ambition if he could only bring off one or two of these most satisfying shots. But how are they to be played? As long as the lie is good, the answer is simple: in exactly the same way as the drive. But supposing the ball to be lying "cupped," the matter requires more consideration. It depends, of course, on the extent of the "cuppiness." When the depression in the ground resembles rather a saucer, and is very shallow, the player will probably get the best result by playing at it as if it were teed, remembering this, however, that he must make sure of getting down to it. The club should go right through with the stroke, and not be driven into the ground and stopped, so as to jerk the ball out. This is a refuge of the destitute, and teems with inaccuracy and broken shafts. But supposing the ball to be badly cupped, it must be sliced out, if any distance is to be gained towards the hole, and this can be done either with a wooden or iron club, provided that the back of the ball is visible, or at any rate part of it. When the ball is so buried that there is no chance of getting at the back of the ball with any of the long distance clubs, the only alternative is to dig it out with the heaviest niblick in the bag. But, apart from this eventuality, a little finesse, coupled with careful watching of the ball, will often coax it out of a bad lie and send it rejoicing towards the hole. The whole of the club face cannot get at the ball, but a part of it can, namely, the heel. Consequently turn the face of the club well up, and get the hands forward at the same time as the body, and slightly drop the right shoulder. This will have the result of drawing the face of the club across the ball and nipping it up into the air. At the same time the slice can be counteracted by swinging the club straight through towards the hole instead of drawing in the arms as soon as the club has met the ball, and by turning the right wrist slightly over to the left. No doubt the more ordinary method of playing the shot is to take an iron and plough through the obstacle behind the ball, and this is a common-sense method of getting over the difficulty. But the former denotes a more finished and a higher plane of golf, and proves that the player who makes use of it has at least one shot in his bag to which the majority of his golfing brethren have not yet attained. Quite as important as the slice shot, which only too many players are able unwillingly to do, is the pull. This is particularly useful in order to hold the ball into a left hand wind, and has also a further merit. It does not detract from the length of the ball and sometimes even adds to it, if the ground is open. For a hooked ball runs in an extraordinary fashion, owing to the absence of cut, whereas a sliced ball, being heavily "cut," drops comparatively dead, if it gets up to any height in the air. The method of hooking the ball is almost exactly opposite to that adopted in slicing. The weight of the body should be carried well forward on to the left leg, and the hands left behind to bring along the club. The right shoulder is kept as high as possible and swings forward a trifle quicker than in an ordinary shot. The hands are kept quite low, and the right hand is rather more on the north side of the leather than in the normal grip. The ball is then struck rather towards the toe of the club and at that moment the right wrist is turned over to the left. The amount of hook can be increased to any extent by exaggerating any of these points; for instance, by putting greater force into the right shoulder, arm and wrist, or by standing more "open," with the left leg drawn away from the ball and the right brought up closer to it. In this way the body swings more easily to the west-south-west, which encourages right-hand play, instead of due west, which is the line of flight of a normal ball. Hooking, in spite of certain advantages, is no more to be aimed at as a permanency than slicing, and the object of every golfer should be straightness rather than length under normal circumstances, but it is a very valuable thing to be able to pull the ball when required. Especially in a strong wind do its advantages most obviously appear. For whereas a sliced shot mounts quickly into the air and soon loses its impetus, the tendency of a ball when hooked is to keep low and to retain sufficient forward impulse to ensure at least a short run when it comes to earth.

What is to be done with a hanging ball ? In the first place a club with a certain amount of loft upon it is a *sine quâ non*. The shot is hardly ever successful with a straight faced driver. It requires a certain amount of skill to steer the flat sole of a wooden club down hill without touching the ground, and the narrow bottom of an iron certainly nips in more easily behind the ball, but with attention and careful watching of the ball, a spoon can be made to do the stroke and the result is much more gratifying. The ball must be cut away, as in the case of a cuppy lie, and the resulting slice can be either allowed for or corrected by turning the right wrist over to the left at the moment of striking. Turn the face of the club

out and bring it down to the ball in such a way that the heel is the point of contact, not the extreme heel, but a spot just behind the centre of the club face. The same method should be followed when a long iron club is used, but it must be remembered, when accuracy in length is required, that the driving power of an iron head is very much smaller near the shank than at the other end, and so the ball must be struck more firmly from there, in order to go the required distance. It is advisable when playing at a hanging ball not to take quite a full swing, and especially not to rise upon the left toe to the same extent as on the tee.

The accompanying photograph gives a good idea of the position at the top of this half-swing. The left knee is but slightly bent, and only the outside of the left foot has left the ground, so that the feet have a

Top of Half-shot (Driver).

[*To face page* 102

very firm grip and the chance of slipping is minimised. At the same time the cumbrous weight of the body is not employed so much, the impetus being mainly imparted by the wrists and forearms, which are at their very fullest tension. The point is that through the shifting of weight from leg to leg the balance is difficult to maintain even on level ground, and obviously it must be a more difficult task when the right foot is at a higher elevation than the left, as in the case of a hanging ball.

This stroke requires great accuracy, and any loss of equilibrium is bound to end in a collapse. But if this stroke is adopted it must be adopted wholly. It must be a real half-shot, and not an easy full one. These spared shots are a snare and delusion. They cannot be played with any consistency. The player thinks that he will bring the club down slowly, and the result is that he does not let his arms out to their fullest extent and the ball is topped. But the real half-shot can be very easily learnt, and its capabilities must be obvious to any one who has seen Mr. Harold Hilton playing it. Be courageous and adopt it. It is a valuable addition to every one's stock of strokes.

When the ball is lying on an upward slope the difficulty is not to get it up into the air, but to keep it straight. Very great care must be taken to hit the ball true, and here again it is wise to rise on the toes as little as possible, unless the slope is very slight, in which case it should be struck as if on the tee. The half-shot will be found just as valuable in keeping an up-lying ball straight as it is in getting the maximum of result out of a hanging lie. It is very important, however, to follow well through and straight in the direction of the hole, as of course the desirability of moving the feet as little as possible only applies to the upward swing, and is in no way an obligation after the ball has left the club-head.

When the ball is lying above the player on a slope facing him, the trend of the ground naturally encourages a hook, and this tendency should be counteracted by slightly slicing the ball in the manner described above. A ball lying below the player on ground that slopes away from him is a source of great difficulty, and no very satisfactory result can be expected. The natural tendency is towards a slice, but this cannot be corrected by hitting off the toe of the club, for the heel is the only part of the face which can be brought into contact with the ball, owing to the bend in the neck. Consequently the best that can be done by a player in this position is to play rather to the left of the line and allow for the slice. This is a weakness which has been discouraged elsewhere, but under these untoward circumstances it is not only excusable, but the only course open. In dealing with balls lying either up against the player or away from him, it is very important to maintain the balance, and so the half-shot is again to be recommended with its comparative immobility of the feet. It is hardly necessary to mention that the ball must be watched with hawk-like eagerness in all the four foregoing shots. There is none of the mechanical swing which is used on the tee, where, within limits, the keeping of the eye on the ball is not so essential every time. These are all emergency strokes and call for the greatest accuracy if they are to be successful, and this accuracy can only be attained by devouring the ball with the eyes.

In all shots played through the green, and for that matter in tee-shots also, it cannot be too strongly urged upon a player to make each shot with a definite view as to the next one. This is one of the many parallels to be drawn between the two great stationary ball games, billiards and golf, though perhaps this affinity has not been called attention to before. For instance, when a strong wind is blowing there is only one easy approach to the hole, namely, in the teeth of the gale. But this is a point which is missed by a large majority of players, and the result is that they often find themselves called upon to play shots of enormous difficulty which by a little forethought could have been avoided, and easy ones substituted in their place. Look ahead to the next stroke to be played, and base the stroke in hand upon it.

Bunker-play is an item in the game, which interests all golfers from the plus four to the twenty-five handicap man. For all alike will at times find themselves in these inconvenient things, whereas certain of the more delicate and difficult shots are not quite within the skill of the long handicap player. Bunkers are legion in their varieties, consisting as they do of every kind of trap which the ingenuity of man or the evil disposition of Providence can devise for the golfer's downfall. But provided that they are in the right places and are not full of stones, that is to say, provided that they are fair, punishing a bad shot but allowing a reasonable chance of recovery, the more bunkers there are on a course the better.

There is probably no course in the world which has enough bunkers, and would not be improved by the addition of more. Bunker strokes differ from all those previously described in that swing is very largely discarded and the shot becomes more of a hit. But it is an important fact, and one which should be firmly established in the mind, that the right application of a little force yields superior results to the maximum of force combined with inaccuracy of hitting.

The classic form of hazard is of course sand, and the method of getting out of this and kindred substances will be dealt with first. If the ball is lying heavily in a sand bunker, the player must be content just to get it out, and hope that a long putt or a mistake on his opponent's part will enable him to get a half. A heavy niblick or mashie is the tool to be used in digging in a bunker. The head of it should be well set back, for there is almost always a face to be negotiated, and the shaft quite stiff. The stroke consists in bringing the club down with as much force as possible, into the sand an inch or an inch and a half behind the ball. The ball must be literally dug out, the sand being the objective to be aimed at, and not the ball at all. The club must be held in the tightest grip, and as much force as possible imparted to the ball without moving the feet. Any attempt to rise on the toes causes the sand to shift, if it is at all loose, and so the stance is altered, the balance lost, and the weight of the body precluded from taking any part in the stroke. The straighter the club comes down into the sand the more elevation the ball will have, and this is a point to be remembered when there is a steep face to be cleared. This is the safe and sure method of getting out of a bunker, and its use should guarantee that the player will emerge from its embraces in one shot only. But there are temptations lurking in every bunker to induce the golfer, when the ball is lying well, to endeavour to retrieve his fortunes by taking a long club. This is a very natural and even laudable ambition, but it should on no account be allowed to clash with the mandate that he must get out in one stroke. It is a question of common sense. In the first place a wooden club has no sort of status in sand ; its broad wooden sole condemns it as unpracticable. For the least touch of the sand in the downward swing and the stroke is robbed of half its velocity. No doubt certain wonderful shots have been played out of sand with brassies and their kin, notably by the late Lieutenant Tait, but the mere fact of their being regarded as portentous, witnesses to their difficulty, and proves that they should only be attempted by the most skilful players, and that too under abnormal circumstances. If any liberties are to be taken with sand, an iron or a driving mashie is the right club with which to make the attempt. An ordinary cleek is too long in the head, and though this objection is shared with the iron, the natural loft on the latter justifies its use. The ball, of course, must be taken quite clean, and to aid this end the feet should remain practically unmoved in the course of the stroke. In fact this is another of the many places in which the half-shot described above gives the best results. Let the player ask himself the following questions before deciding to use a long club in sand. Do the possible benefits to be gained from the stroke adequately compensate me for the extra risks run? Is the ball lying sufficiently well to justify me in confidently expecting a successful issue to the shot? If the player cannot answer both these questions in a decided affirmative, he had better take his niblick and hunch out the ball in the orthodox way. Supposing that the ball is lying well in a bunker close to the green it can probably be pitched out more accurately by being hit quite clean, than by a shot involving much sand. But, to accomplish this, the club must be held very tightly in the fingers of both hands, and the eye must be glued to the ball. For the least touching of the sand spoils the whole stroke.

Another form of obstacle to be found on many courses are whins, "fog," long grass and heather. The secret of success in getting out of their clutches is the same as in all other bunker play. Don't try to do too much. Take a heavy lofting club and play at the ball as if it were lying clear. Hit it as hard as possible without moving the feet more than absolutely necessary, and be sure of getting well down to the back of the ball. It usually pays to bring the club rather straight down on to the ball, for thus the club is not checked to such an extent by the

8

growth behind the ball, and a quicker elevation is imparted to the stroke. But if the bunker patch, in which the ball is entrapped, lies to the right or left of the course, and the green is out of reach, be content merely to return to the fair course, and to get " home " with the next shot. An effort to make a shot of eighty yards out of thick grass rather than one of forty so often comes to grief, and the ball, failing to carry over the whins on to the good turf, falls hopelessly back into the toils. Then, of course, the whole weary business has to be begun again. Nothing is so laborious and trying to the temper as the necessity of repeatedly digging for the ball in really thick grass or " fog."

If a player finds his ball in a ditch, the direction of which is towards the hole, he has not a very difficult task to perform if he elects to play at it. This is, of course, a question of policy, and due consideration should be paid to the number of his partner's strokes, the steepness of the sides of the ditch and the distance from the hole. If he decides to play the ball, the first thing is to get as firm a stance as possible by digging the heels into the banks of the ditch. Then there are two things to be remembered and followed: firstly, not to aim at a long shot, and secondly, to keep the eye on the ball. If the player does not follow the first piece of advice he will almost certainly lose his foothold, and perhaps fall into a muddy ditch. The second point is of course trite, but it has a special significance when the ball is to be struck off mud. For the temptation to shut the eyes altogether is overwhelming, and it attacks the player just as the club is coming down and the contents of the ditch are about to be spattered about the vicinity. Be courageous then. Take plenty of mud, as in sand, and keep the eyes open. It is more likely to fall on your neighbours than yourself, but if you are the sufferer, *tant pis*. It is one of the disadvantages of golf. A ball lying in a cross ditch calls for a decision as to whether the next shot will be made easier by dropping the ball just behind its present position, or by playing it out to left or right. The former is more certain, the latter more remunerative—perhaps. A wooden club has no more status on a macadamized road than it has in a sand bunker. It is impossible to get sufficiently underneath the ball to ensure its rising, and a fear of damaging the sole of the club usually seizes the player at the last moment, the arms are drawn in, and bang comes the horn on the top of the ball. Play with a well-lofted club so as to make sure of getting out of the road, and reserve the recovery for the next shot.

Playing a High Shot out of Water.
(Note the vertical direction of the splash.)

[*To face page* 116.

A ball floating in water is by no means hopeless, and it is surprising what accurate shots can be brought off by the courageous player, who will steadfastly keep his eyes open. Bring the club down about an inch behind the ball, as in a sand bunker, and the ball will sail gracefully out of this alien element without the slightest difficulty. Naturally the "flatter" the club is brought down, the lower will be the trajectory of the ball, and *vice versâ*; so the player will be guided by the length of shot desired in deciding exactly how the ball is to be played. But—and it is a big but—if success is to be anything but experimental, the eyes must be kept open and glued to the spot where the club is to strike, even at the risk of splashing.

Before closing this chapter it may be worth while to say a few words about the cleek and its equivalent, the driving mashie.

This class of club is really a driver except that it happens to be made of iron, and so it should be swung in the same way as a driver on the tee. No doubt it is capable of almost every variety of shot in default of other clubs, and in the hands of an experienced golfer it can be made to play half-shots, to run the ball up from off the green, and finally to put it into the hole. But these are imported accomplishments, and its primary use is for full shots. When these have been acquired the player is master of the cleek. For the supplementary strokes with this club are identical with certain shots with the iron, which will be dealt with in the following pages.

CHAPTER V.

Approaching.—The selection of approaching clubs is a point which needs a good deal of consideration. The clubs to be found in the bags of the majority of good players, or perhaps of all, are as follows: first, a pitching club; secondly, a medium iron, and thirdly, a straightfaced iron. As to the particular form of club to be used, the selection rests upon the idiosyncratic taste of each individual. There are all kinds of pitchers from lofting cleeks or jiggers with thin faces and broad soles to squat Taylor mashies and Fairlie niblicks, with narrow soles and faces almost three inches deep. Every player swears by his own particular tool, and it is idle to attempt to prove that any one class is superior to any other. For the benefit, however, of those who find it difficult to use a Taylor mashie, owing to the liability of the toe to stick in the ground, the following "tip" may be of value. Round off the toe with a file, so that about half an inch of the head disappears. This throws all the weight of the head to the middle, and the bottom of the club can easily nip in under the ball, without any danger of the toe catching in the ground. But whatever club is selected, don't let it be one with a very thin light head, enormously set back. These clubs both look and feel alluring when picked up in a shop, and the purchaser thinks that he would be able to loft stymies with it beautifully. But when he comes to handle it on a course, he will find it worse than useless. He will never be up and rarely straight. Whatever shape the head of the pitcher may assume, the shaft, at any rate, is always the same. It must be quite stiff. This is, of course, the same in the case of all approaching clubs. To use a whippy shaft in these clubs is to court inaccuracy.

With regard to the medium iron there is little to be said. It is a slightly longer club than the pitcher, rather heavier and of course less set back. There is one equivalent to this class of club which to some players may prove a boon—namely, Mill's aluminium spoons, and they should at least be given a trial by those who find the iron a difficult club to use. The noticeable points about these clubs are the straightness which seems inborn in them and the facility with which the ball is dropped dead. The most effective distances at which they can be employed are from seventy to a hundred and ten yards, and when the ball is just off the green. There are two main varieties, short-headed and deep-faced, and long-headed and shallow-faced. Both have their supporters, but perhaps, on the whole, the long-headed type is the easier to play with.

Thirdly, the straight-faced iron. This is a club which plays an important part in the game. It is used for long approach shots up to the hole on an ordinary day, but above all things for playing low forcing strokes into the wind. A wrist shot can be played with this class of club under these conditions, and, moreover, can easily be kept on the line, when a hard hit with a mashie or other lofting club will almost certainly be crooked and short. Mr. J. L. Low, in his comments upon one of the Inter-Varsity matches, says: "A common mistake was the playing of full shots against a gale of wind with a lofted mashie, when the wrist with a straight-faced club would have served. One player, who was a great sinner in this respect, did not even carry a straight-faced iron in his pack." Mr. Low's expression of opinion upon any golfing point is not lightly passed over, and when couched in such strong terms as the above should go far towards proving how essential the club in question is. The three main varieties in use are, firstly, the big-headed, old-fashioned iron; secondly, a deep-faced short-headed club, such as Taylor's mashie iron; and, thirdly, a club which is almost a driving mashie, that is to say, short in the head, but not quite so deep in the face as the second variety. Everyone, of course, will advocate the merits of the class of which they have an example in their bag. That, however, is immaterial. The important thing is to possess some club of this description and to be able to use it. There is one golden rule to be remembered in the choice of the three clubs discussed above. That is, to have the clubs graduated in such a way that a full shot has never to be played with a lofted club. A mashie swung like a driver gives the poorest results. Straightness is sacrificed—for this shot nine times out of ten ends in a hook—and the difficulty of the stroke is increased. For whereas the full shot with a driver is something of a sweep, as in the case of a man scything grass, in a mashie shot the club has to be brought down straighter, and with greater accuracy exactly behind the ball.

The point is, perhaps, best shown by a parallel. It is easier to hammer a nail accurately into a wall by means of a series of short sharp taps of the wrist than by a powerful swing of the whole arm. The clubs should, if possible, be of such a power and capacity that a full shot with one should be equivalent to an easy shot with the one above. For example, a full shot with the pitching club—this expression is, of course, only used hypothetically and as a standard of distance—should be equal to an easy shot with the medium iron, and the same with the two other clubs. Finally, a full shot with the driving iron should be roughly equal to an easy shot with the next club above it, which with some players is a cleek, or driving mashie, and with others a spoon, or brassy.

Experiment will show that full shots with the two lowest clubs in the scale are sworn foes to accuracy, and that more satisfactory and consistent results will be obtained by playing an easy shot with a more powerful club. This, after all, is only a development of the maxim, "Don't under-club yourself," which in turn comes directly from "Don't press."

Approach shots proper then resolve themselves between the limits of the half or three-quarter stroke with the longest iron and the wrist shot with the pitcher. Of course, it is obvious that they are infinite in variety, depending as they do upon the "dance of plastic circumstance."

It is impossible to deal with every class of stroke to be met with on every kind of course. But an attempt will be made to indicate, at any rate, one method by which the ball can be induced to go high or low, to left or right, and to fall comparatively dead, or to run after it has pitched; in a word, the general theory of scientifically approaching the hole.

The longer the shot to be negotiated the more sweep there is in the swing; consequently, the fullest iron shot is exactly the same as the half-shot with the spoon which was recommended in the chapter on

Top of Fullest Iron Shot.

[*To face page* 126.

play through the green. Having assumed a comfortable stance, the club is gripped tightly in the fingers and carried easily back until the club is pointing up into the air at an angle of about forty-five degrees. The left arm is as before, almost straight, and, for all practical purposes, parallel to the ground, the upward tendency being very slight, and the right arm well bent, so that the point of the elbow is about three inches from the body. The left heel is just raised and there is an inflexion of the left knee to the right to ease the swing. The weight, of course, swings on to the right leg, which stiffens during the upward stroke. The club is then brought down with a sweep behind the ball, the body-weight, as before, being shifted to the left leg, immediately before the club gets down. The right shoulder is kept as high as possible and swings well through, thus necessitating the rest of the body doing the same. This is just the ordinary half-shot, and it marks the limit of the iron shot. Any stroke which demands greater length, demands also a more powerful club and should not be played with an iron. The lesser iron shots down to the wrist shot are all played in the same way, except that the club is not taken back so far and the follow through is not so energetic. But the ball should be placed well away from the feet and right elbow kept free of the side. Otherwise the arms cannot get free of the body and, as the club comes down, they are drawn in and the stroke ends in a slice. The ball does not run a great deal off a shot played in this way; for a good deal of backward spin is put on by the mere use of the iron, as is seen by the egg-shaped smear of white paint on the club-face. But the player will soon find out by experiment the normal

Finish of Fullest Iron Shot.

[*To face page* 128.

result of the stroke, and will be able to decide for himself where he ought to try to pitch the ball. If height is an object to be aimed at in these strokes, the club must be brought up into the air as quickly as possible immediately the ball has been struck. This has the effect of spooning the ball into the air to a certain extent, and encouraging it to reach the required elevation. There is no necessity to bring the club down straight, and any excess in this direction more often detracts from the accuracy and length of the stroke than adds anything to its effectiveness. With a short shot of forty or sixty yards, however, this method of hitting the ball high is sometimes useful, when some lofty obstacle is to be negotiated. The club is taken up rather straight, and at the top of the swing, both forearms are parallel to the ground, the wrists being bent back as much as possible, and the club pointing vertically to the sky. The position at the end of the swing is exactly the same, though of course the arms are reversed. The left knee should be only slightly bent as the club goes up, just sufficiently, in fact, to ease the swing and prevent cramping. This stroke, though not difficult to acquire, is not suitable for all approach shots and should only be used in an emergency, when it is desirable to loft the ball to a great height, and then make it fall dead on the green like a poached egg. The normal stroke, however, is to take the club back fairly flat, and a sufficiently high trajectory is attained, provided that the wrists bring the club-head up from the ground as soon as the ball has been struck. To keep the ball low and induce it to run after it has pitched demands, of course, exactly the opposite treatment. The hands should be kept quite low during the whole stroke, and the club-head pushed straight through as close to the ground as possible. The right wrist also should be turned well over to the left at the moment the stroke is made, and the ball hit slightly off the toe. This naturally gives the ball a bias to the left, of which account must be taken, and the shot should be aimed a little to the right of the hole.

It is often of great value in playing shots on to a green to make a use of the wind to assist the stroke. Of course, when playing into a head wind, the ball should be hit perfectly true and straight. But when the wind comes either from the right or left, a judicious employment of a small slice or hook well repays any time spent in acquiring these niceties. The ball is, of course, sliced into a wind from the right and hooked into one blowing from the opposite side, the result being that it is not only not deflected from the line, but it is robbed of much of its forward impulse, and, therefore, encouraged to fall dead, owing to its prolonged struggle with the adverse wind. In fact, much the same effect is produced as when the ball is hit directly into a head wind. The method is much the same as in all intentionally sliced and pulled shots, though the amount of bias imparted to the ball is, of course, infinitely smaller than in a full shot. To slice, keep the right hand rather under the handle and hit the ball slightly behind the middle of the club, drawing the club face across the ball. To pull, hold the right hand well over the handle and hit the ball towards the toe of the club, keeping the hands low. It must be remembered that only a slight spin is necessary, and that if the ball is unduly hooked or sliced it overcomes the resistance of the wind and a crooked shot results.

Finish of Low Forcing Shot (Iron).

[*To face page* 132.

As to pitch shots, it does not seem really to matter how they are played. As in putting it is important to move the body and feet as little as possible and to hit the ball clean. Provided that the player does not hit the ground before the ball, he can be sure of taking his putter for the next stroke. The grip of the club should be quite firm to prevent the club face being turned off the line of the stroke, especially when the shot is played out of a heavy lie. It is very common to see these shots missed, owing to a loose grip and to the wrists not being "creamed up." Don't be afraid of taking the club well back. It can be brought forward slowly if the stroke is a very short one, and this part of the business can be safely left to the instincts of the wrists. To strike the ball by taking the club-head only a very short distance back, and then flicking it forward by a sharp twitch of the wrists, is to adopt a very difficult and uncertain method. There is a jerk as the club begins to come forward, and the player's head in consequence is often thrown into the air, the eyes being removed from the ball. Take the club well back, and remember that the more slowly it is brought forward, the more the ball will be lobbed up, and, therefore, the more likely it is to fall like a poached egg. In order to play short shots with success the player must have a very definite idea in his mind as to how he is going to play each one—that is to say, whether he will run the ball, or try to pitch it more or less dead. This, of course, depends entirely on external circumstances, the nature of the green, the lie of the ball and so forth. Go forward at least half the distance of the stroke and look at it from this point. A correct impression is thus obtained of the requirements of the stroke,

A High Pitch Shot.

[*To face page* 134.

its distance, and the nature of the ground to be traversed. Further, it is usually easier to get into the hole from one side than from the other. Consequently ascertain on which side the easiest putt is to be found, and play deliberately in that direction.

This is only one more application of the maxim that every stroke should be played with a view to making the next one as easy as possible. In fact, it is merely common-sense.

CHAPTER VI.

Last of all comes putting, the most difficult, as it is the most effective branch of this complex game. It seems so unfair that a little tiny stroke of six inches or less should count the same as a magnificent drive of two hundred yards. And yet it does, and, moreover, it is more often that short putts are missed than these epoch-making shots of which the golfer is so proud. Probably the reason why it appears so much more difficult than the rest of the game is that any inaccuracy causes a definitely missed putt, while in the other shots, even though the ball is not hit perfectly, at least some progress has been made towards the hole and a possibility of recovery is still left open. In fact the result of a player's errors is brought more forcibly before him on the green and consequently his distress is more poignant. In the first place putting is *not* an inspiration. Success in this branch is the result of enormous care, and either consciously or unconsciously doing certain things, which give the best results. No doubt on certain days, Providence determines that every ball shall go into the hole; but consistency in putting, which constitutes real excellence, is not obtained by any external aid. There are occasions, unfortunately rare, in which certain isolated long putts fill the player with perfect confidence, and he is absolutely certain that this particular putt will be holed out. Why this is so is impossible to say, nor, indeed, does it matter. It is a phenomenon which calls for explanation from the Psychical

Research Society rather than from the golfer, who can only be thankful when it is vouchsafed to him. The reason, however, for its success is not hard to find. All doubts are resolved in the player's mind as to how the ball is to be hit, and the result is that the hand and eye work together in perfect harmony. He is reduced for a moment to the state of Adam in the Garden of Eden, who, it is reasonable to suppose, would have been an excellent natural putter. How else can one account for the man, who comes to watch and says "It looks easy." He takes his umbrella, tries a putt, and almost invariably holes out the ball. He has perfect confidence in his power to do this simple thing and a certain contempt for the man with the bag of sticks, who performs it so irregularly and with so much posing and inspecting. It is only when he tries a second time that he fails. For then he has fallen under the spell of the game. He is not quite so confident, and the ball somehow does not go down. Short putts especially are made very much easier by means of confidence, and a stock of this commodity should be kept at hand for use at all times, whether it is a spontaneous growth, or of a spurious quality, pumped up to meet the necessities of the moment.

So much, then, for what may be called the psychological side of putting. The practical part is what really matters and it will be dealt with at greater length. Firstly, the stance. This position of the feet does not matter in the least degree. Good players are often to be seen altering their stance in two consecutive putts. The only point of importance is to stand firmly and comfortably, so that there will be no danger of losing the balance, whatever motions the arms may choose to indulge in.

Secondly, the grip. There is much to be said for bunching the two hands together into one big hand or unit of force. By this device the player is saved from the difficulty of discriminating which of the two hands is the master, and he does not find one pulling one way and the other another. But it is in no possible sense essential, nor does it find favour with all players.

It is important, however, to hold the club firmly at the moment of striking the ball. A slack grip produces sloppy putts. The club is not under sufficient control, and consequently comes down uncertainly, sometimes touching the ground, and at others striking the top of the ball.

The dominant hand in putting is the right, because it contains what may be called the putting nerve. The sense of touch is to be found between the second and third joints of the first finger, and the ball should be hit from this joint. In all games the touch is imparted to the ball by this finger, with the exception of cricket, in which the ball is struck from a V formed by the thumb and first finger. This, however, is the sole exception, and in every other game the fore finger plays the important part. Consequently, whatever grip is adopted, let it be one which allows the forefinger of the right hand to crook itself round the club in such a way that the last word with regard to direction and distance rests with it.

The ball should not be placed too close to the feet, unless a very upright putter is used, especially for a long putt, when the ball has to be struck fairly hard. For it is difficult to take the club back the required distance without the arms coming into contact with the body, and this is apt to upset the aim and spoil the stroke. Place the club behind the ball, the exact spot with which the ball is to be struck being exactly opposite to the centre of the ball. Then arrange the body and arms and feet so that the club has its natural lie, or, in other words, so that the whole length of the sole of the club is resting on the ground. In fact the club is held in its most natural position, without any cramping or discomfort. The vast majority of players bend both the knees when putting. This encourages an easy pose, and helps to keep the balance ; but the really important thing is to keep the whole body absolutely still, not rigid, for that introduces rigidity into the arms and spoils the aim, but firmly and easily balanced on both feet, and—once more let it be said—comfortable. In the actual stroke as little movement as possible should be set up in the body. As has been said before, it is easier to exercise absolute control over one fraction of the body than over the whole. Consequently keep the unemployed part quite quiet, so that it can be disregarded, and confine the attention to accurately moving the part which makes the stroke. This is really the right arm. The left plays only a very subordinate part, its function being to steady the stroke rather than impart strength or direction to the ball. The power is mostly derived from the right elbow and its immediate vicinity, the right wrist contributing a certain amount; but the point to be emphasized is that the putt is a right-handed shot. After the actual stroke the player should follow through with the club. The ball should not be tapped, or, worse still, jabbed, but rather swept along towards the hole. There are two points of recommendation in bringing the club-head well through after the ball. Firstly, the ball is more likely to run smoothly and truly on its course if this is done, whereas a tapped ball is apt to spring sharply off the club into the air and so be deflected from the line. Secondly, if the club is taken through, it is not necessary to hit the ball so hard, for a great deal of run is given to the ball by this process, and, consequently, it is not necessary to give it such a vigorous blow. The harder the ball is hit, the more difficult it is to keep it straight. This is a universally accepted fact, and from it the advantage of the follow through is patent. It is, however, essential to make the club-head follow the ball exactly along the line to the hole, not so much in order to make its influence felt as long as possible, as to ensure that the ball is hit true and without cut. For if the club-head is found to the left of the line at all soon after the ball has been struck, its position proves conclusively that the face has been drawn across the ball and the shot sliced.

The omission of this straight follow through is at bottom the reason why such a large majority of long shots with a wooden putter go to the right of the hole. This is a phenomenon which is very noticeable, and by some golfers has been considered so far incurable, that they deliberately aim to the left of the hole.

To putt well it is necessary to form a standard by which the player can judge, unconsciously no doubt, how much force is to be put into the stroke. In other words, the ball must be struck every time on the same spot on the club face. This is a very difficult thing to do, requiring constant care as do all repetitions, witness certain tricks of this nature on a billiard table. The attention is deflected for a moment from the matter in hand, and the stroke is missed. It is natural to choose that part of the club which has the greatest driving power, a spot which is located just in front of the exact centre of the club. With a wooden putter there is every encouragement to hit the ball from this spot; for it is clearly defined by the fact that the maker usually stamps his name on the back of the club exactly opposite to it. With an iron putter, however, there is no such mechanical aid, and constant care and watching of the ball is necessary to ensure striking the ball correctly.

Another point to be noticed in acquiring a standard is the necessity of hitting the ball every time without touching the ground. This is done simply and solely by keeping the eye on the ball, a platitude, of course, but one which cannot be too often reiterated. Sometimes the eye is tempted to follow the club-head on its backward journey. This it does with success, and the club is seen at its furthest point away from the ball. But as soon as it begins to come back again, the eye outstrips it in its eagerness and plunges forward, with the result that the club-head follows it and digs into the ground. For the eye is a false counsellor on this point and the result is a half-way putt. More commonly, however, the eye is carried forward before the ball is struck, and during this period when its authority is relaxed anything may happen. The ball certainly may be correctly struck, and very often is, but, on the other hand, it may equally be tapped, hit on the heel or toe, or the club may touch the ground. Always watch the club-head meet the ball, after having carefully assured yourself that the face of the club lies exactly at right angles to the desired line of putt. It has certainly been advocated that in very short putts the player should look at the hole rather than at the ball.

Of course a putt of a foot or eighteen inches, although theoretically bristling with difficulties, is not really a very severe test of skill, but it cannot be doubted that its difficulty is greatly enhanced by removing the eye from the ball. The player cannot be *certain* of hitting the ball true and on the right spot, if he is not looking at it, although it is probable that he would hole the putt nine times out of ten, if he were blindfolded. Short putts need just as much care and attention as their longer brethren, and though haphazard tapping may answer brilliantly one day, method and diligence, with a dash of confidence, produce the best results in the long run. Take plenty of time about a putt and don't permit the desire to get the stroke over to get the upper hand. Having thus acquired a standard, by examining the ground over which the ball is to travel, a shrewd guess can be aimed at as to the requisite strength to be put into the stroke, in order to drive the ball up to the hole. When the ball has to be putted over a slope and allowance for small depressions and hillocks has to be made, the player should be quite clear in his mind whether he will play the shot slowly, trickling the ball, or whether he is going to hit firmly at the back of the hole. For the line of the putt is different in these two cases. A gently hit ball requires more "borrow" from the hill and *vice versâ*, just as in bowls the bias makes itself felt to a greater extent when the speed is reduced than immediately upon the projectile leaving the hand. It is well then to decide how the ball is going to be struck before deciding what is the correct line of the putt under consideration. Another great point about putting is at least to start the ball fair. It is, of course, impossible always to emerge a victor over "the malignancy of inanimate objects." The player can only do his best in this unequal struggle and the result lies upon the knees of the gods. The ball is often deflected by small inequalities of the ground —too small that is to be allowed for—but obviously it is something gained in a long putt if the ball starts on the line. This is best done when using a putter with an absolutely perpendicular face, by turning the head a trifle up in the air, so that an element of loft is given to the stroke. The player, however, must be careful not to cut the ball, or, if he does, to correct the slice by striking the ball rather on the toe, or by slightly turning over the right wrist to the left. If a putting cleek is used, this difficulty is not encountered. For there is a little natural loft on the club and thus the ball naturally is given an upward tendency when struck. Perhaps, however, it will be enough, if the player abstains from smothering the ball. There is a pernicious habit prevalent among golfers of pressing the sole of the club into the ground, just before the backward part of the stroke begins, and in the same motion turning the face of the club slightly down. Whether this pressure is an infringement of the rules of golf or not is immaterial in the present context, but it is difficult to see what benefit it confers upon those who use it. On the contrary, it seems to have an actively detrimental effect. For the tendency is to hit the ball into the ground immediately in front of it, whence it may continue its course to left or right or straight with absolute indifference. Moreover, a ball hit with the face of the club turned over rarely, if ever, gets up to the hole. A smothered ball is a limp ball, and it is obviously a harder task to calculate the direction and distance of a ricochetting shot as this becomes, than of one which is clean hit.

"Always try to hole your long putts." This is the advice which Mr. A. F. Macfie has got to give on the subject. The player, when he gets on the green, must not be content merely to run the ball up somewhere in the direction of the hole. He should take all the means in his power to make the shot as accurate as possible. If there is any question as to the line of the putt, the player should go to the hole and look along the ground at the space over which the ball is to run. For some reason, though its exact nature is not quite clear, the line can be gauged far more accurately when viewed from this point than when the putt is examined from the ball, and when two lines seem to be indicated the correct one is always that which is shown by examination from the hole. Having satisfied himself what is the direction of the putt, the player should go back to the ball, and, after his usual preliminaries, hit the ball along this line. But he must have the courage of his opinions and use the course recommended to him as right by his eyes, when they examined the putt, even though it may appear improbable from his position near the ball. If a player finds himself hooking his putts, this defect can very often be set right by holding the right hand rather more underneath the handle, and the contrary also holds good as a remedy for slicing. Perhaps, however, the commonest cause for these errors from the straight line is that the club-head is not originally held at right angles to the line of the putt. This is a point which must be carefully attended to in each putt. For on it much of the accuracy in direction depends. Aim as a general rule at the centre of the hole, remembering, however, this, that all putts are essentially right-handed strokes, and that the tendency of the right hand is if anything to pull the ball round to the left. This being the case many players will find that it pays rather to aim at the right-hand edge of the hole in any but very short putts. For thus the slight disposition towards hooking is remedied without any alteration in the grip. In any case the right edge is a better objective than the left, for as has been repeated *ad nauseam,* a slice is an abomination, whereas a hooked putt runs very true and is rarely short. In putting, as in every other branch of the game, consideration must be paid to the next stroke, if the chances of holing the putt be small. Examine the lie of the ground round the hole as in a short pitch to discover from which side it is easiest to hole out, and then even if the aim is not actually directed towards the point, the player will do well to remember what is the result of his examination, and, the will being father to the deed, he will unconsciously hit the ball towards the desirable side of the hole rather than to the other. This, of course, is of no value when the putt is for the half, and indeed only comes in in long putts which are unlikely to be holed, but there are circumstances which sometimes arise in which it proves a useful hint. One more tip about approach putts may be of value to those who have not seen Mr. Low on the green. If the shot is long and the distance consequently difficult to estimate, divide it into two equal parts by standing half-way between the ball and the hole. It is extraordinary how much these strokes are simplified by this manœuvre, and a far more real idea of the work to be done is thus conveyed to the brain than a glance from behind the ball could ever hope to confer.

Stymies, the only remaining difficulty upon the green, really need no explanation. They are a common-sense question. If the stroke to be played is for the half, the situation calls for desperate measures. The player will probably find it easier to loft his ball over his opponent's than to put on sufficient slice or pull to squeeze round the obstacle and into the hole. The knack of pitching the ball is easily acquired, and is practised assiduously by many golfers. Consideration should of course be paid to the lie of the ground and the wind before a decision is arrived at. But this is purely a matter of weighing probabilities in each individual case.

When the adversary has played the odd, and the stroke is for the hole, the same risks need not be undertaken. There is almost always a safe half awaiting the pawky golfer, whereas a very little inaccuracy may give away the hole by the player putting in his partner's ball. Again, it is a question purely of probabilities and of the daring or prudence of the individual. *Chacun à son goût.*

CHAPTER VII.

Among the natural points necessary for the formation of a good game, temperament takes a very high place. It is obvious that of two players who hit the ball equally, or almost equally, well, the winner, accidents barred, will be he who possesses the temperament best suited to golf. In order to test his natural capabilities, let the player ask himself the following questions, and if he can honestly free himself from the imputations contained therein, he may rest content that mentally, at any rate, he is a fully-qualified golfer.

1. When did I last, on missing my drive, accuse the caddie of teeing the ball badly,

instead of facing the fact that my bad shot was due to nervousness or pressing or to my error of judgment in not seeing that the ball was teed right?

2. Am I in the habit of saying, "That would have been a good shot if it had been straight," or—worse still—"That *was* a good shot, but the wind got it"?

3. When my ball, having clearly pitched in a moist place, has stopped within two yards of where it fell, am I tempted to remark, "I cut that one pretty heavily"?

4. When, though playing well, I miss a shot badly, can I forget all about it by the time the next tee is reached?

The points emphasized in these questions are two in number, and they are really the two essentials in the golfing temperament, firstly, the power of facing facts, and, secondly, self-control.

Without these the golfer lays himself so

open to invidious comments in the club-house, and his friends make such good use of the opportunities supplied to them, that it is a marvel that he does not speedily see the error of his ways and reform. But from the frequency with which one hears remarks of the class quoted above, it would appear that reform is a plant of slow growth, and that the temptation towards self-justification even by these most unconvincing means is too strong to be resisted by the genus golfer. When a man has played a bad shot, why should he say anything at all? A dignified silence seems to be indicated as the best course. But if the occasion imperatively demands that something should be said, let a man acknowledge honestly and with a good grace that he has made a mistake. His opponent has seen the shot, and consequently will not be convinced even by the most specious excuses.

But, on the other hand, he will not. in all probability lower his opinion of his companion's play, nor will he be tempted to laugh, whereas feeble excuses are almost certain to excite ridicule.

Another point connected with this subject is that of talking. In no game is the golden nature of silence more strikingly shown than in golf of a serious nature. Of course this does not apply to a friendly match, when the game is regarded more as a medium for conversation than anything else. For although the contention that "if a game is worth playing at all, it is worth playing as hard as possible," is surely right as a principle, the individual exceptions to it are almost as numerous as the case in which the principle asserts itself. But serious golf is best played in silence, or at any rate with as little conversation as possible. A man must fulfil the wishes of his opponent without criticism or resentment. It does not do to play tricks with other people's nerves. If both players are really interested in their match there is no necessity to cry the score after every hole. It is only too well known to the man who is "down," and the winner is no doubt congratulating himself inwardly on his present advantages, and planning how he may increase it in the immediate future. Again, congratulation of one's opponent upon good strokes and sympathy with him in misfortune are better left unexpressed. If the match is a tight one there is too much personal interest to make such remarks absolutely sincere, and they convey very little real meaning to the recipient of them. Of course these are mere pinpricks of annoyance compared to the hopeless exasperation caused by a really garrulous partner. The following is a conversation which all golfers must have heard in some form or other. "Well, how did you get on?" "Oh! I bore it till the turn, and then he simply talked me out of the next four holes, and that finished me"; or perhaps, "He groused so infernally about my good luck and his bad lies that I could play none after the first few holes." No doubt these are avowals of weakness on the part of the loser, but sufficient troubles and trials are provided for the golfer in the course of the round without the addition of this crowning torture. Besides, when all is said and done, golf is a game, and as such demands to be played in a sportsmanlike way, and incessant talking to the detriment of one's opponent's play is in no whit a more venial matter than moving about on the putting green when he is engaged upon an important shot. Fortunately, however, the talking golfer is apt to cut his own throat by this very failing. For it is impossible for a man to talk and concentrate all his attention upon the game, and it is just this very concentration which is an essential attribute of sound and successful golf.

One more point is worthy of mention, and that is confidence.

A man should never allow himself to be overawed by his opponent at the outset, just because he has got a good reputation. This is seen happening again and again at cricket, especially in school matches. A good bowler comes down and, although bowling very moderately, dismisses a whole side for quite a few runs. And the reason for the failure is simply that the batsmen have got it into their heads that they can't make runs off this man because he played for the Gentlemen three years ago. It is exactly the same thing at golf. Good players often play badly, and if their opponents can only bring themselves to remember that the match is merely the test of which of two men can play the greatest number of good shots, and not a contest between a lion and a mouse, the *soi-disant* mice will often find themselves victors, albeit somewhat unexpectedly, at the end of eighteen holes.

Confidence, moreover, makes the short putts go down with surprising regularity, and further enables a man to "hang on" at the end of a tight match, provided only that he regards his opponent as a man of like failings with himself.

The golfer, then, whose aim it is to win his matches, is advised to start with the conviction that he is going to win, even, or perhaps especially, when the odds are against him. There is no need to express this forecast in words; in fact, it is extremely unadvisable to do so. But let him just nurse the conviction privately, and he will find it of great service when the pinch comes, as it usually does, about four holes from home.

Finally, if a man who has begun golf casually, and without teaching thinks it worth while to try to radically improve his game, he must be content to get worse before getting better. Such a man has probably several hopeless faults which effectually prevent him from reaching any but a low standard of efficiency, and these he will have to give up altogether and accustom himself to a different set of motions. While this process of transition is in progress, the player's game is certain to deteriorate, but provided that he has a good teacher and sufficient stamina to persist, he will certainly emerge from the ordeal a better and more consistent golfer. Consequently rivalry of a certain kind is a distinct bar to the acquisition of a good style. A finds that by slogging round in his casual and unorthodox way he can have consistently good matches with B, and if this is his highest golfing ambition, let the matter rest there. But if he aims at something higher, he will have to go through a period during which he will continually have to put up with defeat—a particularly irksome state of affairs—until his patience is rewarded by turning the tables not only on his old rival B, but upon others of his golfing brethren, whom previously he had regarded with unmixed awe and admiration.

———

PART III.

Training

The Golfing Temperament

The Aluminium Spoons

BY

H. G. HUTCHINSON

TRAINING.

THE acts of heroes carry with them great responsibility. Once, many years ago, a very heroic professional golfer of St. Andrews imbibed freely over-night of the bowl that when taken freely does not fail to inebriate, and on the day following he won the championship. On this insufficient dictum the professional golfing youth of St. Andrews, and elsewhere in Scotland, based a system of training which was piously followed by the majority of them for several years. It cannot be argued with any justice that they failed to grant the system a fully adequate trial. Nevertheless, experience has proved that it is not perfect. It has been proved, more than once, that it is quite possible to get ever so drunken over night and yet not to win the championship on the morrow.

Another system has come into vogue, and the most successful of the professional players of to-day are virtually teetotallers. There is not the least doubt that excess in the drinking of alcohol, in the smoking of tobacco, and so on, have evil effects on the nerves. This is a fact as patent as any maxim of the copybook, but the most obvious maxims are not always followed as they should be. On the other hand, if a man is a habitual drinker—not a drunkard—and a habitual smoker, probably there would be no wisdom in his giving up alcohol and nicotine altogether on the eve of a big match. Probably such a radical change would work as big an upset of his nerves as a heavy drinking bout. The conclusion of the matter most likely is that you want to come to the tee in the best of your normal health, not in any abnormal condition. Perhaps to this end you may moderate your amount of drink and smoke a little. I do not think you should do more.

A man must be fed to play golf. It is ill going golfing on an empty interior. A famous St. Andrews professional said once: "The only difference that I see between Mr. L. and Mr. H. and the professionals, is that they get mair to eat and mair to drink." And a good thing too—for their golfing.

Eat and drink, therefore, in moderation, but sufficiently, and as to other kinds of training, they have to be taken up with caution. I do not think that any good is to be done by such things as a gymnastic course of Sandow exercises. I remember

Mr. Tait saying to me after he had been going through the work incidental to his gymnastic instruction course, "I do not know how it is; I am certain I am stronger than I was, but I cannot drive as far." And another player, of less fame, who had apprenticed himself to Sandow for a while, told me just the same. They get into a condition that they call "muscle-bound," or something of the sort, from these exercises, and though they get fearful strong, it is not the right sort of strength for a quick hit. The fibres get too solid and slow. There is a nice phrase of Chaucer's that conveys very well the sort of activity rather than strength that is wanted for the best striking of a golf ball. He speaks of his young squire as being "wonderly deliver"—spell it how you like. The "deliver" expresses the idea of all the strength concentrated on the instant of hitting the ball better than any other phrase I know. Unhappily, it is archaic and obsolete. The one form of exercise that I think might be good is with the kind of dumb-bell that is used to strengthen the grip. This, used with the left hand especially, might be a help.

For the rest, of course anything that aids in getting rid of any rheumatic stiffness must be useful, for we want to be as supple as the stress of years will let us be. Naturally, however, the best of training for golf-playing consists in playing golf—in practice. Willy Park, the ex-champion, once said to me that no man could rely on playing his game unless he had played every day for six months. N.B.—Park is a Scot, so of course this reckoning excluded Sunday. But, even so, what a heroic reckoning it is. Obviously it suits better what Mr. Lawrence Lockhart called "the professional children of wrath" than the amateur who plays the game for pleasure. But without making a toil of the pleasure it is possible to put in a good deal of practice, and perhaps more intelligent practice than the golfer often takes. Practice, indeed, in its proper sense, the average golfer very rarely condescends to. He will go out playing matches day after day, round after round, till it becomes to him a veritable "white man's burden," but of practice, in the sense that a billiard player understands it, he takes no heed whatever. There seems to be a curious likeness, which may be profitably considered, between golf and billiards. It is a fact quite notable that in the recent amateur championship tournament held at Hoylake, amongst other remarkable things in the competition the finalists were men of whom neither had learned golf as a boy, one, certainly, the ultimate winner, was at least a decade, perhaps two or even three, older than the age that we look on as the prime of golfing life, and both these finalists were very far above the average amateur at billiards. Mr. Fry has been billiard amateur champion. To Mr. Hutchings a fifty break is an unconsidered trifle. There are other instances in plenty of a combined faculty for these two games, golf and billiards, which have in common the big fact that the player strikes a ball that is at rest.

When a billiard player—that is to say, a man who really wants to improve his game—says he is going to practise, what does he mean? He means, I think, that he is going to set to work to try to get the mastery of a certain stroke or certain succession of strokes, to make a break. Generally it used to be the spot stroke that was practised most, but it may be nursery cannons, or it may be the middle pocket, or what you will. In any case you will not see the billiard player of any intelligence knocking about the balls without some method in his madness. It is just this kind of practice at a particular stroke for which a golfer hardly ever has the patience or the inclination; but it is just this practice that is likely to be most useful to him. One of the chief reasons, I believe, that Mr. Fry has been so wonderfully successful as a golfer is that he has applied to the out-door game some of the methods of the in-door. I am told (I have not seen it, but I fully believe it) that Mr. Fry would often, at one time, instead of playing a game of golf, take out a dozen balls or so, and spend all the morning practising approach shots from forty yards or thereabouts. As a probable consequence he is, I think, better at this distance from the hole, more likely to hole in two, than anybody; and it is just this that makes him so bad to beat. Surely this must be the right way to practise—to practise particular shots and particular clubs—especially those shots and those clubs that are giving most trouble at the moment.

The ordinary golfer, if he goes out with a club at all, when he is wandering over the links, generally takes a driver. It is such fun seeing the ball go, with a good hit. But probably the driver is just the least useful club to practise with at odd moments, because it is the club with which you get most practice in a match. It were much better to take your brassy, with which you do not get one-half or quarter as many shots, or your cleek—in fact, any other club than the one you do take. But men, especially golfing men, are quaint things. They will continue taking out the driver to the end of the piece.

And then you hear them ask whether it is any use practising putting. Surely they are not so misled by the phrases of a maxim-monger as to accept *au pied de la lettre* his dictum that "putting is an inspiration"—a something that it is almost sacrilegious to meddle with or attempt to improve on. There is nothing so very different in learning to putt at golf and learning to pot at billiards. Then go to John Roberts and ask him whether it is any good practising, if you want to learn to pot the ball with confidence, and see what he will say to you. His answer will not be a compliment to your intelligence, but it will be a convincing one. Golf too, like billiards, is not a game of miracles, it is a game of hand and eye working together in a harmony that is acquired by assiduous practice rather than by any other means, and by an assiduous practice of the strokes in which you are most weak and in the strokes which are most important. And you will not say that the putting strokes are among the least important.

It is not by *tours de force* that games, except very occasionally, are won, but by great certainty in the strokes that are frequent and easy. And it is just this certainty that practice gives.

THE GOLFING TEMPERAMENT.

WITHOUT a doubt the ideal golfer, like the poet, is born, not made—we speak for the moment less of the quality by which keen eye and hard muscle work in harmony, than of that subtler business of temperament which counts for so very much in the soul-searching game of golf. A man is born with a temperament, the gift of his ancestors, of certain quality, and if that was the disposition that was going to serve him (or be of dis-service to him) throughout his life there would be no more word to say. But the truth is not thus. Man does not go through this vale of tears and bunkers with his inherited temperament unmodified. Every student of the metaphysics, from Aristotle down to the latest who has failed to improve on Aristotle, is satisfied that the temperament of the man of discreet years (that is to say, of the ripe golfing age at which grandfathers now win amateur championships) is made up of qualities inherited *plus* qualities personally acquired, and that there is value in the formation of a good habit or ἠθός.

The game of golf is rather like the rest of the game of life (only that it is infinitely more important) in that it is chock full of injustice. Allan Robertson, oft-quoted sage, said it was "aye fechtin' agen ye." So like life—yet more important than life, for no failure affects so keenly as the missing of a short putt on which the result of a match turns! There are so many occasions for exasperation—there is such a lot of good luck (that it is to say, your opponent's luck) in the game, and such a lot of bad luck (that is your own) that really it seems more, sometimes, than a sensitive soul can endure. Aristotle, and no doubt Allan Robertson would be with him, admits that there are some woes that are too heavy for human nature to bear, and which justify resort to suicide. It seems that there are many occasions in golf justifying the golfing suicide of "never touching a club again." You determine, a thousand and one times, that this decision shall rule all your future life. In the morning you are up, eager and fretting to be on the tee again.

Aristotle, or another of equal wisdom, has written that "if you lose your temper you will most likely lose your match." There are exceptional cases of men who seem really nerved to greater and more successful effort by an access of rage. But they are very exceptional, and the rage needs so firmly controlling that perhaps we should call it by some other name. And shall we rather call it "dourness," the eminently Scottish frame of mind in which the Lowlander achieves great things. That is one of the forms that control of temper and of the innate passions—the pettish and spoilt-child passions—assumes. It is not the most pleasant form, but for certain temperaments it is perhaps the only way possible of confronting "the stings and arrows of outrageous fortune." The most pleasant form of all belongs to certain natures—let us take Scottish instances, since we have said that the less pleasant is characteristic of the nation that gave us golf: let us instance "Old Tom," of whom Lord Moncrieff (I think it is) writes that he was "born in the purple of equable temper and courtesy." In his case *nascitur* is the word. So too,

I think, of the late Mr. F. G. Tait. He had a natural sweetness of temper that a bad lie or a long putt holed by an opponent could not sour. It is not given to all to have these sweet qualities by nature. The point to realise is that strenuous endeavour may go far towards their acquirement. It is very hard for one who is of the conditional temperament supposed to be the peculiar attribute of the artist, to control his feelings, to keep his temper sweet and to keep on trying when every moment he is tempted to throw his clubs away in a pet, to curse his fate and his caddie, and to burst into tears. But a deal may be done, as the metaphysicians have pointed out, even with the most unfortunate materials, by forming habit. If a lark sings unconscionably loud, so that no man can putt, affect not to hear it. If your caddie hiccoughs on the stroke (my own always hiccoughs at the thirteenth hole—unlucky number), disregard it. An immense deal is to be done at golf by suggestion—self-suggestion. If you tell yourself that these things, these distractions, do not matter, do not affect you, by degrees they actually will cease to have affect. Treat them as the Christian scientists treat pain—that is, other people's pain—say it is all nonsense and does not exist. That is the right recipe. On the other hand, if you let yourself cultivate the continual habit of watching for occasions of distractions, soon it will become too strong for you to fight it, even with your best efforts. It is just like a temperance lecture.

Of course, determination and effort can do a very great deal, but I believe that the power so strikingly shown by a few of rising to the height of a great occasion is a gift of the gods, and not to be acquired. Still a semblance of it is to be acquired, and many of its results achieved, by a resolve to go on trying, even when fortunes look most desperate. If you go on trying up to the bitter end, always, then—once out of every ten times say—fortune relents, rewards your efforts, and you snatch victory from the jaws of catastrophy. Perhaps, rightly understood, this is really what rising to the emergency means. In the calculation of chances it may come out that once in a while the unexpected event will happen; but it will happen more often if you give it a fair chance by trying your best. Even if you fail, you have done much by the mere trying, for you have a precious knowledge that you have done your best, and also have laid another brick in the edifice of forming your habit. All this counts, even if it fails to win the present match.

And after all that is said, and even though golf is such a game as it is, it is not wholly inconceivable, on the other hand, that things may go unexpectedly well with you. It always is right to be prepared for the unlikely circumstance. In this circumstance, too, the value of the strong control is very apparent. One of the players in the last amateur championship said to me: "It is terribly upsetting to find yourself suddenly two or three holes up on a man you expect to be beaten by. I never can knock out a good man," he said; "I always can knock out a bad man, even if he is playing ever so much better than the good man." I liked this. A man who can realise his weakness so fully has gone far to conquer it. The right way would be (as Goethe conquered his dizziness on a height by often going to the top of a tower) to play often with a better man—only you first have to catch your better man. But the remark was full of insight. If you or I, brother duffer, went out with the name and fame of Harry Vardon, Harry Taylor, or James Braid upon us we should find our opponents much easier to beat. It is almost as hard to play the winning game as the losing. It requires great command of nerve. I believe the better way, if you find yourself up on a stronger man to go on pushing at him, trying constantly to get more and more up, playing in as light-hearted a way as you can. If you get playing too much for safety you are rather apt to fall on disaster. And never make the mistake of not trying to hole a holeable putt because you are a few up. Do not content yourself (unless the green be fearfully keen or sloping, or the wind very strong behind you) with lying dead. Keep on hitting a man when he is down is the right way to play golf. Otherwise you never know when he may jump up and hit you. And just as you ought to keep trying your hardest right up to the finish, so ought you to begin trying your hardest from the very start. Give your man no peace ; keep him moving.

As for score play, it is altogether abominable, but at times a necessary abomination. Here you have to beat not one opponent, but all opponents. You are alone against the world. All the maxims of hardihood are required in greater measure than in match play, except that you do not have here the man-to-man fight, the personal magnetism does not come in. Every golfer, probably, has some one or more *bête noir* of an opponent against whom he finds it very hard to do his best (I do not speak, of course, of those whom you suspect of intentional designs to put you off by playing on your sensibilities—they are outside the pale, and should not be played with) and who beats him constantly. I think we should deal with him as Goethe did with his mountain vertigo—keep on playing with him until the sensation wears off and familiarity has bred contempt.

Human nature is so funny, and it is such a thousand pities that neither Aristotle nor Shakespeare was a golfer. There is no other game that strips the soul so naked.

THE ALUMINIUM SPOONS.

THE man who made the maxim that putting was an inspiration said further that iron play was a science. Driving he claimed to be an art. Of course these brevities, that are full of the soul of wit, do not bear expansion and examination. All the golf strokes are a form of art, in that they are practically applied knowledge. The golfer does not care for these logical subtleties, but commonly (not always) he is subtle enough to perceive that there is a difference between the art of iron play and the art of other strokes at golf. There is a difference in the means. The iron stroke proper you play with a cut down on the ball, that takes up a fid of turf—a practice which vexes sorely the soul of the ancient baffy-playing golfer who fails to realise that his scruffing at the turf with his wooden club does a deal more harm than a solid divot taken out. The divot can be, should be, replaced. The scruff of the "baffy" is blown into irretrievable morsels. The "baffy" however is, for some—that is, for those who have not acquired the specialised art of iron play proper—a far easier weapon than the iron or the mashie. You play this "baffy" approach stroke in just the same straightforward way, with the club following through straight after the ball, that you play a drive or a putt. There is no cutting down on the ball, there is no new art to learn. Now there are a great multitude to whom anything like a fair mastery of the iron shot seems an impossibility. And failure in a shot of this kind is very fatal; because the club is descending, is not going along over the surface of the ground, but down into it; and in consequence, if the ground be taken, only a little, before the ball, the club sticks in the ground and hardly says anything to the ball at all. In fact, the foozle is hopeless. In the stroke with the "baffy" there is not the same margin for error, nor the same need for exactness. The stroke is a straightforward one, therefore there is so much the longer distance of the arc it describes during which it may meet the ball fairly. There is all the difference between playing forward with a straight bat and a crooked, at cricket. You have much more chance of meeting the ball. Undoubtedly there are many people to whom the proper iron shot presents vast difficulty, and all these would do a great deal better with the old "baffy" spoon.

Until about a year ago there would not have been the slightest use in writing all this. It would have been waste of words. The use of the "baffy" was looked on as equivalent to a confession of inability to play the iron—a humiliation to which no self-respecting golfer would stoop. But about twelve months, or a little more, ago, Mr. Mills appeared on the scene, following up his aluminium putter with his aluminium spoons. The guileless golfer "caught on" at this new invention, and has taken to the spoons quite kindly, without a notion, generally, that he is really only reverting to the old time methods of the days before iron play became general. The aluminium spoons go in gradation of loft of face and length of shaft from a club that is equivalent to the modern brassy down to one that in every particular, except the unimportant point that the head is of aluminium instead of wood, is the old "baffy." Of the longer aluminium clubs it is only to be said that they fulfil quite adequately all the functions of the brassy, cleek, etc., according to their respective lengths; and of the "baffies" the merits have been indicated in the above disquisition on the value of the old wooden "baffy" to those who are not very skilful with the iron or mashie. They have the obvious additional merit of being less subject than wooden clubs to wear and tear. It seems possible to use them with a greater loft of face than can be used with any certainty on the iron clubs, doubtless because the straightforward nature of the stroke tends to make tolerable accuracy more easy. There are certain strokes for which they seem peculiarly well adapted, and from a good lie they will pitch a ball very dead indeed. Even some of the most skilful iron players use these clubs with advantage in some circumstances, and it is quite possible and easy to use them alternatively with irons and mashies. The strokes are perhaps so wholly different that the one does not in any way affect the accuracy that a player may have attained at the other.

If one may presume to give counsel it would be to all and every player as follows: "If you have a club for approaching that suits you well and that you can use with fairly certain effect, by all means stick to it; but if not, and if you find difficulty in the use of the approaching irons, make trial of the aluminium spoons, for they are likely to play the stroke for you far more easily."

Part IV.

For Parents and Guardians

CHAPTER I.

FOR PARENTS AND GUARDIANS.

Golf, happily, is made, not for the few, but for the many; and though the vast proportion of us will, in all probability (playing as we do), never reach even a single figure handicap, most of us who have any proper spirit, and a good conceit of ourselves, hope some day to be much better than that. It is this spirit which prompts our secret and carefully-concealed delight when our handicaps are lowered, though most likely we say bitter things about the committee. Across the excited brain of even the least sanguine of us there flit dim glimpses of what it must be like to start from scratch. Now to soberly hope that one will some day be a scratch player is a very excellent ambition, but most people with the best intentions, and very considerable perseverance, seem to the present writer to go the wrong way about attaining it. For it is a gift only given to the few to guess intuitively the right way of doing things; these are they who wrangle among themselves for the open championship. But most people, if left to their own devices, will naturally tend to do things either quite the wrong way, or, anyhow, the way that is wrong for them. For in golf (barring a few little details, such as generally keeping your eye on the ball, and as far as possible not hitting it absolutely on the top when a long shot is required) there are no absolute laws. Some day, perhaps, there will arise a man who never looks at his ball. Then, if we are wise, we shall say that one more fallacy has been exploded. But (if we are wise) we shall not attempt to copy him. Parents and guardians, for whom this is written, must all keep their eyes on the ball if they wish to hit it. There is no possible exception to this rule.

Now in the preceding portions of this book J. Braid, Mr. J. A. T. Bramston and Mr. Horace Hutchinson have all said a quantity of extremely interesting things, in which the scratch golfer will certainly find much profit, if he attends to them. But for babes (though they are parents) these great giants have put forth strong meat. J. Braid, for instance, on his own confession hits with the utmost possible force of his wrists just before the driver touches his teed ball. He is certainly right in attributing to that the immense length of his drives. But if the average player of fourteen-handicap who has played golf, let us say, for years, and in his soberer moments despairs of ever reaching single figures, attempts to hit as hard as he can at the end of a full swing, he will probably miss his ball altogether, top it, slice it to cover-point, pull it to mid-on, or merely play the husbandman with the tee. In fact, there is scarcely anything that he will not do, except hit it true. If by special interposition of Providence he does hit it true, it will certainly carry a longer distance than it otherwise would, but the chances are that (given a player of this calibre, one, in fact, who has not reached a single figure handicap with years of practice) it will not be hit true. And hitting a ball true is for everybody always and for ever far the most important thing in the game.

It is the case of this fourteen-handicap player that it is the purpose of this chapter to consider. He is, we will suppose, extraordinarily keen on the game, an assiduous practiser round about the last green while waiting for his match, and a constant player, who averages his four or five rounds a week, taking holidays and work together. When he is at work, however, he does his work properly as a man should, never has a club in his hands for a moment, and never has considered it possible that there could be such a thing as golf-practice in his bedroom for five minutes when he is dressing. On the other hand, when he does get away from town for his day's golf, and, above all, when he is on his holidays, he plays the whole day, a single in the morning, a foursome after lunch, a single after tea, and as likely as not he will have a handful of balls to drive or play with his mashie on to some unoccupied green in spare moments. But in spite of all this practice, although he has a good eye, and no inherent defect for the game, he does not improve, and is surprised and pained at it. The pain is inevitable, and he has our sincere sympathy for it, but the surprise is totally illogical, for though he plays so much he is doing nothing of an improving nature. For he does not keep his hand in on those days when he is not playing, he plays far too much on the days when he is playing, and, above all, the so-called "practice" which he so pathetically takes is, in all probability, only confirming and strengthening his already existing faults and vices. As for teeing six balls and driving them in rapid succession, he could not adopt a more certain way of learning to drive improperly. By the time he has driven three he will be fatigued, though he does not know it, and the fatigue is only momentary. Consequently the fourth, fifth and sixth balls will almost certainly be discouraging excursions.

Again, though he considers, and rightly, that a match is the fun of the game, yet if he at all seriously wishes to improve, these three matches a day, especially if played as he probably plays them, are the last things in the world likely to be good for his game. For in each case he naturally wants to win the match which at that moment occupies him, and he has for certain in his bag some club, a mashie, let us say, which is behaving in a childish and impotent manner. In consequence, whenever he can he will avoid taking it out; he will putt over rather rough ground near the green, when he knows quite well that the mashie was the right club to use, could he only use it; or, if he is still some ninety yards off, he will play improper iron-shots. Now this policy may prevent his losing this particular match, but if persevered in will go a long way towards losing him many others. Instead of having improved his mashie-play, he will merely have let it establish a funk; and, as far as practice is concerned, his day's golf has been pure loss. Again, he may be playing with a far-driving opponent, and his inclination will be to press. To-day the result may be satisfactory, but he will not have improved his driving.

Again, since he wishes to improve, he will very likely have lessons from his club-professional. Now though many professionals are admirable teachers for those who have in them the makings of scratch players, they are not always so good for those who at present show no very marked aptitude for the game, and for those who count their years by the double score; for they do not always, as is natural, considering their own skill and facility, make due allowance for the frailty—or, indeed, the strength—of thick-set and elderly people. A long loose swing is a sheer physical impossibility for an alderman. Many of us are modified aldermen; we should, therefore, probably do well to modify the swing also.

But the mashie practice, the half-dozen balls lofted on to the unoccupied green? Is not that certainly a good practice? Emphatically not, unless they are lofted in the right way, or anyhow, unless an attempt is made to loft them in some definite way, with clear notions about where they are wanted to pitch. That is what the average player will not trouble to do. He plays a succession of what we may call "general shots"; he means them to rise in the air a little, and to run a little. Thus the first shot may be fairly successful (*i.e.*, it may be played more or less as intended), the second is most successful and lies nearly dead, but instead of being fairly lofted (which was the design), it is skimmed over the ground, with long run and little rise. And the assiduous practiser will be delighted with the shot, and feel that he is really improving with the mashie. As a matter of fact, he has merely made an absolute fluke. He proceeds. The third is lofted high and falls without much run; the fourth pitches just short of the green, but has a long run. And so forth.

Now on the face of it, this sort of proceeding looks like practice, because the player is hitting balls with clubs; in reality, it is nothing of the kind, and though it is probably good even to have a club in your hand, and the feel of the ball on the blade, it is certainly bad to practise in this slovenly manner. Moreover, the player probably selects with care excellent lies for the balls he purposes to loft. Unfortunately he cannot do this in a match, for it is against the rules of the game. His whole method of practice is wrong from beginning to end. Much can be done with a mashie and a handful of balls, but not thus. Instead, let him take his handful of balls and drop them on to the ground. They will by the law of gravity roll into any little hollows and depressions there may be about. It is into these that they will roll when he is playing his match ; it is that initial difficulty he has to contend with. Then let him look at the general lie of the ground ; let him imagine the perfectly played shot, no general shot, but a definite particular one, pitching from a certain height on to the place from which he judges that the run of the ball, *as he means to play it*, will take it right up to the hole, where it will lie stone dead. It is the image of that shot that he should think of when he has taken his stance in what is for him *a natural and comfortable attitude.*

Now this natural attitude, which Mr.

Bramston has insisted on for everybody, and is doubly necessary for parents and guardians, is one of the foundation stones of success. One sometimes hears a man say, "I am always uncomfortable over that sort of shot"; and the moral is that he should devote his mind for the present in seeing how he can play it comfortably. Not only does a natural attitude, provided it implies no vital error which produces a bad stroke, give the best results in all cases, but it is also the base of what is known as style, which, if attainable, is certainly desirable. For style means to the man who knows nothing about it, apparent facility, to the man who possesses it, it means real facility. And facility is a thing most certainly worth cultivating, since to find any class of stroke difficult is to start heavily handicapped in the matter of nervousness. For golf, like most other games, is largely a matter of confidence. Who, for instance, does not know the frequency with which a putt goes down if one is only quite clear in one's mind that it is going down?

Provided, then, that out of the million possible methods of playing a stroke, one comes easily and naturally to a man (particularly a parent or guardian), and there is no sure and inevitable disadvantage in playing it that way, he will probably be right in practising the stroke in that method, and not in the method of anybody else. But he should be quite certain what that method is, and not consider that a "general shot" is any use at all. The first general shot may finish near the hole, the second, though played with the same intention, may also finish near the hole, but after a run instead of a pitch, or *vice versâ*. But the practiser, instead of being complacent, should consider that he has made a thoroughly bad shot.

It is as much a fluke, in fact, as cannoning at billiards off a couple of cushions when the direct cannon was intended. No doubt, several of the balls which he has dropped in order to loft on to the green will have very different lies, and as such should be very differently played, but each should be played with intention. It is this stroke, we think, of all others—a shot from forty to sixty yards on to the green—that improves most surely with practice, provided the practice is of the right sort, and, on the whole, it is the most paying shot in which to attempt to attain proficiency. It is often said that every game between two fairly evenly-matched players is fought out on the putting green, and that the man who takes only his average of two putts on the green is, if he is anything of a player at all, nearly unbeatable. There is no doubt a good deal of truth in this, but we shall get even nearer to absolute truth if we extend the radius a little, and say that it is by the short game generally, the mashies and putters, in fact, that every match is decided. And the short game is, luckily for us, exactly the game where the most elderly can attain proficiency, whereas not all the practice in the world could possibly enable them to make a really long drive. No doubt a long drive is the most fun, but there are thousands of golfers who never could, never can and never will drive a long ball. But many such are very formidable opponents, because they have attained excellence in those departments of the game when excellence was within their reach. It is, therefore, to the short game, of parents and guardians, that these chapters, after a few remarks about the drive, will be devoted. To arrive, however, at the short game, it is necessary to have got within reach of the hole, and the start must be made from the tee, with this proviso, that everything here said is meant to be of possible value to none but those whose drives are usually both short and erratic, and will not be of the slightest interest or profit to any decent driver at all.

Now it seems to us that for people who have taken up golf late in life when suppleness was passed, the full swing, especially when it is combined as in really long drives with very hard hitting as well, is practically unattainable, and it is far more important to be able to hit the ball fairly from the tee on most occasions than to hit it well once and badly three times. The occasional long shot may, even more occasionally, win or halve a hole, but what of the three others? Screamers are charming things, but they do not happen to everyone, and to practise them is one of the most obvious ways of wasting time. But a certain mediocre usefulness from the tee is not to be despised. Anyhow, it is better than feverish topping, and those of mature years and comfortable figure will be wise to consider whether a shortened swing might not help matters. For if by a full swing (or as full a swing as is humanly possible) they do not get a really long ball, and at the same time are very unsteady, it is worth seeing whether a shortened swing, though it no doubt shortens the length of their very best drive, will not help to secure a drive of greater average length and straightness. But it is most important to make no attempts to shorten, or in any way interfere with, the follow through. For though it would appear that it cannot matter what happens to the club after the ball is on its way, such a doctrine is both practically and theoretically utterly wrong. Indeed, it would almost be truer to say that the follow through is the only thing that does matter. For, apart from question of underspin, which will not here concern us, the length of any drive is wholly dependent on the velocity with which the club-head strikes the ball; and it is impossible, if the club is moving with any considerable velocity at the moment of striking, that it can be brought up short immediately afterwards, for the velocity cannot be instantly checked, and if it could the club would instantly break. In other words, if a man has a bad follow through, it implies almost for certain that he has begun to check the club before the ball has been struck, and that, therefore, the club is not moving with its greatest velocity then. The same thing is true of putting: tap the ball only and you will be more often short than not; follow through and you will be more often up than not, though, as far as you are aware, you played the two shots with the same strength. In itself, of course, it is perfectly true that when the ball has left the club we can do anything in the world without interfering with its carry, but the follow through is the test, the criterion of what has gone before. Supposing the club is moving with fair velocity there will be a fair follow through; it is when the club has been checked before the ball has been struck that the follow through is bad.

Now with a shortened swing, where the club-head, let us say, at the top of the swing is not much higher than the shoulder, it seems only reasonable to suppose that there are less opportunities for inaccuracy than when it is brought completely round over the back behind the head; the liability to error has not so wide a field. At the same time, it is almost more important that the club should be brought back slowly in a short swing than in a full swing, especially if the driver shaft is at all whippy, since in the short swing there is less time and space for the bending of the shaft, which is caused by a quick back, to readjust itself and let the face of the club strike the ball fair; and though you cannot come forward too quickly, yet you cannot go back too slowly. Also just as in a full swing, the curve the club-head describes should be as flat as possible; the ascending and descending curves which it makes should not be steep. As Mr. Horace Hutchinson has pointed out, a very up-and-down movement of the club leaves practically no margin for error, since the club-head is travelling (given the ball is fairly struck) in the same plane as the ball at one point only; whereas in a flat curve it moves for several inches in the same plane as the ball. This holds good, of course, in the short swing, as well as in the long, and in the short swing an additional reason comes in—namely, that the weight and force of the shoulders, which bear a greater proportionate part of the stroke, are more easily and naturally employed if the swing is flat than if it is upright.

It will be seen at once that this stroke is necessarily more of a hit than a swing. It is exactly for this reason that we recommend it to those whose anatomy is not adapted for swinging, but who have very likely plenty of hitting power, in the hope that they may find that they will, with a little practice, find that they gain enormously in accuracy. It is true that they will probably sacrifice a few yards of their best drive, but there will be fewer real foozles, and certainly far fewer sliced balls; and of all bad balls the sliced ball is the commonest. They will find, in fact, that if they adopt their usual stance they may have a slight tendency to pull, owing to the increased work done by the right arm. If this pulling is at all serious, it can easily be avoided by standing a little more open, drawing back the left foot or advancing the right. But if they find that the hook is never more than slight, above all, if they find that they are acquiring any control over it, and by an alteration of their stance can accentuate or diminish it, they must remember that they are acquiring a stroke of great utility, and not throw it lightly away for the sake of straightness. For a slightly pulled ball is, as James Braid has said in an earlier chapter, the only method of getting a long drive in a severe cross wind from the right; and though this attempt is perhaps another risky experiment for the average fourteen player, yet a slightly pulled ball is the longest ball on the course for everybody, and to have moderate command over a pull is an acquisition of value. And this seems to come naturally to those who shorten their swing while retaining the ordinary stance. However, it is better not to pull it out than not to know where you are going to, and the pull can be avoided as we have said by standing rather more open.

Now though the upright swing should not be employed unless necessary, sometimes it is the only means by which the ball can be hit fair. This is when it is lying with an inequality of the ground rising immediately, or nearly immediately, behind it. Here, to strike the ball at all, it is necessary to "nip in" between the excrescence and the ball. This cannot be done with a flat swing, for the club-head would in its natural course merely hit the excrescence and be stopped by it, or slid off on to the top of the ball. But in such a lie many parents and guardians adopt a proceeding which is lamentable in its effects. They first of all allow themselves to feel irritated with the bad lie, and then hit for all they are worth "in the hope of something happening," a hard "general" stroke, in fact, of fatal results. They think vaguely that they may hit the ball clean, in which case it is all right, and they will have had the satisfaction of a long ball from a bad lie; if, on the other hand, they do not, they blame the lie, and say it is scarcely worth while playing on a course like this. Of course a ball may be badly cupped, or lie so immediately close to an excrescence behind it, that it is practically impossible to get a decent length out of it. But if that is the case, take a niblick, or at most a lofted iron, and make the best of a bad job. But three-quarters of such balls, of which we all have our share, are not so bad as this; and though it is annoying to lie badly after a good shot, you will find that the results of a wild "general" shot will not, in nine cases out of ten, allay your annoyance. What is to be done then? Firstly, if you feel any real distrust of your wooden clubs in such a juncture, humbly take an iron of some kind, for it is in shots like these that two things are absolutely necessary—care and confidence. Hold the club slightly shorter than your wont, go back upright with the intention of nipping in with the club-blade between the offending lump and your ball, and, above all things, go back very slowly and steadily. From the nature of the lie there is only one point at which your club can meet the ball; except at that one point it cannot be travelling in the same plane. So above all things, do not hit hard and wildly. The limits of correctness here are infinitely smaller than when you are driving from the tee with a flat swing.

Now here is a shot which can be confidently recommended to the attention of the patient practiser. It is not a stroke which presents any difficulty that should rightly be considered insurmountable by the ordinary mediocre player; but, take it all round, there is scarcely another shot on the links at which the ordinary mediocre player comes so regularly and consistently to grief. When he is confronted by it he instantly assumes two wrong attitudes, one of the mind, the other of the body. Mentally he says to himself, "I have got this lie off a good drive; it is impossible to play against such luck." His body thereupon reflects this rebellious attitude, takes the wrong club and plays in the wrong manner—wildly, that is to say—in hopes of "something happening." Something usually does, and fids of the unoffending county in which he happens to be, fly dumbly protesting in all directions.

Now a little practice (four or five shots at a sitting is as much as is good for anyone) will do wonders with this shot. To be in the habit of purposely placing a ball in such a lie goes far to correct the instinctive annoyance of finding it there in the course of a match, while the habit of playing extremely careful shots when one has laid such a ball for oneself goes even further to correct wild hitting when the adverse fates lay it there for you. The universal instinct of parents and guardians is to hit very hard and consequently unsteadily at such a ball, in the hopes apparently of (i.) hitting it clean after all; (ii.) cutting through the solid ground behind it. But if (i.) is aimed at, why hit wildly? If (ii.), why not take a niblick?

But the shot is not uncommon, it is also rather difficult. That is why it is worth practising. *Only* a very accurate shot, the club travelling downwards so as to strike between the ball and the lump behind it, will be any good. Hit wildly from the tee if you like: that is far easier. But do not hit wildly here.

Another lie where an upright swing is useful is when there is a rising bank in front of the ball, over which it is necessary to get the ball, when a heavily lofted club like a mashie will not carry a sufficient length. Here, by this upright stroke additional underspin is put on to the ball, which causes it to rise quicker than it naturally would, and the obstacle surmounted, the player will reap the benefit of the carry of the longer club. In this stroke, it may be observed, all the intention of following through is there, though no actual follow through happens, since the face of the club, after the ball has been struck, is checked by the opposing rise of the ground. The shot is not a very difficult one, and it is often of great value. In it, as in the shot before, confidence is given, and so probably accuracy, by holding the club rather shorter.

Though probably most players of the standing we are considering would be unwise to try to slice and pull intentionally, they find that there is plenty of slicing and pulling in their game without any intention at all; and though it may not be of use to them to know how to obtain it at will, it will certainly be of use to them if they can learn how to cure it. The methods of the slicer are manifold; he arrives at his stroke in various ways, but always *viâ* the fact that he puts the side spin which makes a ball break in from the off at cricket on to the golf ball. Drawing his arms in just before he strikes the ball will give him this undesirable result, for the face of the club will thus be drawn across the ball from outwards inwards, causing it to rotate on its own axis. So, too, he will slice if the toe of the club is turned outwards, so that it does not meet the ball square. Again, if he stands very open—*i.e.*, with the right foot much in advance of his left, he will tend to slice, or if in making the stroke he gets his hands in front of the perpendicular of the club. But whatever he may be doing, it is of the first importance that he should find out what he is doing. If, for instance, he is drawing his arms in, he will not remedy matters by attempting to turn the toe of his club inwards, or altering his stance. Some players, though indifferent performers, have an excellent eye for their own and others' faults, and know when they are doing wrong, though they seem unable to correct it. Others, again, though good golfers, if they fall into a bad habit, seem utterly unable to see what it is. It is, however, much easier to see what another person is doing wrong than to see what you are yourself doing wrong, and your opponent, or, at any rate, your caddie, will probably be able to tell you. Then, having ascertained your fault, you will probably find that you can correct it most quickly—an important thing in a match (but only to be used for the time being)—by cultivating for a stroke or two the opposite fault rather than the right way of doing things. For instance, if you are turning the toe of your club out and so slicing, do not at the next stroke attempt to lay it square to the ball, but try to turn the toe in, so that in ordinary circumstances you would hook it. The reason for this is that on a slicing day your tendency is to turn it out, although your intention is to lay it square to the ball. Thus if your intention is to turn it in, the result will, we hope, be that you lay it approximately square. In the same way with regard to stance, if you find that you are on any given day taking up too open a position, deliberately get into one which on your normal day would give you a hooked ball—that is to say, advance the left foot and draw back the right rather more than you think you usually do. But, above all, if you have on any given day a tendency throughout to commit a fault, do your utmost during the game to prevent your mind dwelling on it. For the fear of a mistake in golf brings with it the mistake; if you say to yourself, "I must not go into that bunker, but I am afraid I shall," you will very likely go there. But if you say, "I must carry right to the edge of the green," though you may not do it, you will have minimised the danger of the bunker. The same perverse phenomenon occurs in the early stages of bicycling: to dwell on the fact of a ditch means to finish in it.

Finally, with regard to the long game generally, as opposed to the short game, it is most necessary to play with the head. How often does it happen that in the attempt to carry a bunker, which we have no reasonable chance of carrying, even though carrying does not mean we are therefore on the green, we gravely take a driver and go deep into it, whereas two moderate iron shots would have made us reasonably certain of getting on to the green in the same number of strokes. The scratch player, who is a really long driver, might get there in one, and so perhaps might we, the fourteen handicap folk, if on this particular occasion we drove our very best ball. But even the scratch player is taking risks, and we in our futility take more than a risk. Yet round after round we elect to "go for" hazards which we cannot really expect to carry, knowing in our own hearts, even as we stand addressing the ball, that the best we can hope for is to top it violently, so that the next shot may be within reach of the green. Of course, if there is a really reasonable chance of getting on to the green in one, attempt it by all means, or if your opponent is already there and you have to get there or lose the hole. But in general, if you consider that your average shot will land you in trouble, be firm with yourself. Play within your limits, and get going at the short game as favourably as possible, instead of beginning it from the bowels of the bunker.

For with regard to the long game in general, it is to be remembered that all things considered, you will win more matches by playing the long game fairly and the short game well than *vice versâ*. The reason is simple: for in the ordinary round there are more strokes of the short game played than of the long. Even in what we may call a driver's course where a long driver can reach many of the holes in one drive or two, or perhaps three, yet the longest driver of all will make mistakes, and even then there is the putting to be done. Take, for instance, the first hole at Sandwich, in which a good driver will green himself in two, while our two best shots will perhaps just reach the bunker guarding the hole. But he in all probability will not have laid his second close to the hole, whereas if we are near the green with our seconds we have a certain chance, if we attend to our short game of putting the mashie shot within holing distance. Besides, we are certainly receiving strokes, and there is a far better chance of the stroke coming in, if we play the third from easy distance off the green than if we delve at it, probably unsuccessfully, from below the cliff of the bunker.

All this sounds pawky advice; pawky it is, for golf is a pawky game. J. Braid goes, quite rightly, on different lines, and says he wins more holes by going for hazards which are about on the limit of his carry than by playing short. But we unfortunately are not J. Braid, and it would be as foolish for us to follow his policy as it would be to attempt to hit as hard as he does. Such things are his *genre*; for us they would spell disaster.

CHAPTER II.

THE SHORT GAME.

It is very hard to define what is a putt and what is not. Some people would say that any stroke played on the prepared green is a putt: others that only strokes within twenty yards of the hole are putts: others that only strokes played with putters are putts. But in the first case, the hole may be close to the edge of the prepared green, and there is a matter only of a yard or so of smooth rough between us and the prepared green. Or in the second case there may be a bunker within twenty yards of the hole; does therefore the violent niblick putt for us, for it is ill if it does? Or in the third case some people never use a putter at all, but play with favourite old irons. It is more convenient therefore, since such wide difference of opinion exists, not to attempt any definition, but treat the combination of mashies (sometimes irons) and putting together, calling it the short game, as opposed to the game where distance is the object aimed at, and where you play the stroke with the full power of your club. Nobody, for instance, ever putts as hard as he possibly can, though there are those who play with the mashie sometimes as hard as they can. These go to the left.

The long game then, generally speaking, ceases at the moment you cease to play full shots. At this moment maximum distance ceases to be an object, and then all that has to be done is to play the shot with *requisite* strength, the strength required being within your power. If you can only estimate the required strength correctly, and play the shot precisely as you mean to play it, you will always, when you are within reach of the green, hole out in one. You will also be able to give, provided you are moderately competent with your driver, about two strokes a hole to every living golfer. This is a beautiful and encouraging reflection. But mashies and putters are fickle folk, and must be taken in a far more serious spirit, if anything is to be done with them.

Professionals, quite rightly, and all good players of the game, are for ever telling one to be up with the first putt. It would be a good thing if they extended this advice, and told one to be sure to be up with the approach stroke from off the green. It is a far commoner fault, in fact, with most players of only second-rate ability to be short with their mashie than too far with it, thus leaving themselves a putt right across the green, or even another mashie shot. If they have observed their own play attentively they will probably have noticed that if they attempt to put cut on to the ball they are apt to foozle. Consequently they forget that every mashie shot, when it is fairly and squarely hit, has a certain amount of cut on it, from the loft of the club. This, when the ball pitches, checks it slightly. In consequence most people are short with their mashie, not by four or five feet, as is the case with the first putt, but by four or five yards. In the long run this makes a great deal of difference, for it leaves to the average putter a putt which he cannot reasonably hope to hole, instead of one which he may.

Now there are almost as many methods of using the mashie as there are mashies, and there is only one which for the individual player is right, and that is the one which he finds easiest. To drive a very long ball off the tee it is certainly necessary to use the wrists, but there is no one method of using the mashie which can be predicted for any one player. But, for the parent and guardian, it may be said that as a rule it is better not to try to put on cut. Anyone can do it, but the stroke, like the Matterhorn, is dangerous though not difficult. A small error if the ball is cut is productive of worse results than if it is not. In other words, it is easier to estimate the probable run of an ordinary shot than the effect that cut will have on it, even supposing (which is most improbable) that the amount of cut which is intended is put on to it. There are, of course, some cases, to be treated of presently, where it is necessary either to cut the ball or to lose the hole. These, however, though not rare, are special rather than general.

A great rule about mashie-play is, if possible, to pitch the ball on the green. Clearly this is not possible, if to pitch the ball on the green implies running very far from the hole, or overrunning the green altogether. But allowing for the possible slope of the green, it is obvious that the shot will have a better chance of running straight, and that the approximate length of its run can be more easily calculated if it is pitched on a *soi-disant* uniform surface, than if it is pitched on the rough. Dreadful things may happen to it in either case, but dreadful things are more likely to happen if it is pitched on to an uneven surface, than if it is pitched on to an even surface. Therefore, when possible, pitch on the green, provided that the extra risk of putting cut on to the ball is not necessary to keep it near the hole. This will also help to correct the universal tendency not to be up. Avoid, therefore, a low running shot which has to skip about at the mercy of the unstable elements before it reaches the green, if it is possible—without cut—to pitch the ball beyond their incalculabilities, on the comparatively *terra firma* of the green itself. Thus the risks will be minimised, and Heaven knows we have enough of them when the mashie is in hand. But before the green is reached, distance has to be traversed in the practical security of the air, for, given there is no wind of consequence, a ball is much safer there than on the ground. The question is how to get the ball firmly into the air.

In the short game much more than in the long—except when the sun is in our eyes and the temptation to look up and dazzle oneself as well becomes almost irresistible—there is a tendency to take the eye off the ball before it is fairly struck. It is probably due to the fact that the hole is close, and we so intensely hope to see the ball slowing up or pitching close to it, that we look up to see if it is there before it has really left the club. Be this as it may, many more eyes are taken off putts and mashie-shots than off driven balls, and with equally fatal results. Let it be our aim therefore to continue anxiously to look at the place where the ball has been after it has quite gone away. It is no use really looking at where it has been when it has gone, but it will save us from looking up before it has gone. Almost any snap-shot of a mashie stroke, if taken at the right moment, will show the player's eye glued to an untenanted blade of grass. In any case it is no use looking up with mathematical exactitude the moment the ball has gone, and it is quite certain that if your habit is to do this you will sooner or later

—probably sooner—look up before the ball has gone. In this case it is unlikely that you will see it where you wish to. Therefore take precautions, even if they seem over-cautious, against this particular temptation.

It is almost, if not quite, impossible to lay down any rule whatever about the correct stance for mashie play, for the distance from the hole at which it is used should be always well within the full shot of the club, and thus the problem is not how to get the utmost possible out of the stroke, as in driving, but how to avoid pulling, slicing, topping or getting underneath the ball. The first and last are easily eliminated, since almost all pulled mashie-shots are full mashie shots, which should never be played at all, while, unless the ball is lying in soft, tussocky grass, it is not common to get underneath it, since there is no temptation, it is not a full shot, to fall over the ball.

Topping and slicing, on the other hand, are extremely common faults, but unless there is exceptional difficulty in the lie of the ball they ought, even for parents and guardians, to be very rare. For topping, in the majority of cases, is due to taking the eye off the ball, even though the player may think that he has not done so until the ball has been struck. But he will probably be conscious of having looked up, as he would say, quite immediately afterwards, and in such cases we take the liberty of believing that he is wrong, and has really looked up before. Another cause of topping is from the very common habit of looking at the top of the ball, whereas it should be borne in mind that a mashie-played ball is hit (if successfully hit) on a spot quite out of sight. This is the case, of course, even in a ball driven through the green, but more so in a mashie, for the lower edge of the blade of the mashie is at the moment of striking tucked away underneath the ball. Therefore, should a fit of mashie-topping come over you, and you are humbly satisfied that you are not letting your eye wander from the ball, it may easily be productive of good results to look not at the ball while addressing, but at a blade of grass immediately behind it. Slicing again, as in driving, is due to turning out the toe of the club, and is perhaps most often caused by letting the heel of the club touch the ground before the ball is struck. It is exceedingly easy to do this, especially if the player takes his stance at too great a distance from the ball, and the effect naturally is that the blade, so to speak, pivots on its heel, letting the toe turn out; a slice is the inevitable result. It is most easily cured by taking especial pains when addressing the ball to bring the blade close up to the ball, and see that it is quite square to it, to go very slow back, and to stand rather nearer to the ball. Often, of course, there may be some impediment: in a rough lie or on heathery ground, for instance, or among bents there will often be some wiry stalk immediately where the heel of the club must come. In such a case the only thing to do is to grip the club very tightly with both hands, so as to check the tendency to turn which must invariably happen, and to remember that an obstacle has to be overcome before the ball is reached. It is then necessary to hit rather harder, or swing the club rather further.

Probably all good players regulate the length of their approach shots by the length of their backward swing. This is, beyond doubt, the sound and safe thing to do. On the other hand, all of them probably at the last moment hit with their wrists, adding this to the swing, and it is this combination of hit and swing which most players find so difficult. The wrists, it is certain, are strongly brought into play by any one whose mashie work is passable, and the right moment for them to work is immediately before the ball is struck. Every one knows the empty feeling with which he regards his tired ball barely reaching the lower edge of the green, though he feels sure that he hit the ball true and devoted to the *whole* stroke sufficient force. In these cases what has happened is that he has put his wrists into the shot either too soon or too late: their force, that is to say, has spent itself before the ball is reached, or it comes into play after the ball is gone. Of the two faults, that of bringing the wrists in too soon is probably the most common, for the muscles of the wrists are very quick workers, unlike the larger body-muscles, which are meant to support or for comparatively slow movements, and the *curve* of the wrists is a flick. Thus it is at the last possible moment before the club-head meets the ball that they should be applied; they should not be turned over gradually on the downward stroke, but flicked over. This also causes the ball to rise more quickly, and lengthens its carry in proportion to its run. That is to say, it will in the initial yards of its flight clear obstacles which would stop it if the shot were played without the flick of the wrists, and it will enable the player to pitch the ball further than he could otherwise have done without over-running the hole. In other words, he can often pitch a ball on the comparative uniformity of the green, where he would otherwise have had to pitch it on the rough and trust more or less to luck in the matter of awkward kicks; in fact the two shots may be paralleled by the high lob of a howitzer as compared with the flatter trajectory of a 4.7.

Of course this wrist-work has its dangers, just as it has its rewards. The blade of the club, as will be obvious, is turned in a far more lofted position to the ball if the wrists are, when the ball is struck, in the middle of their flick, and it is therefore harder to judge how far its energies will result in height, how far in carry. But there are many occasions on which, as for instance when there is some obstacle near the ball which must be lofted where a quick rise is essential, and many others, when length of carry and shortness of run are highly desirable. This can be secured in an even higher degree by a further refinement of the mashie-shot, which, though it bristles with difficulty, is yet interesting. This consists in deliberately drawing the club during the stroke *across* the proposed line of flight of the ball instead of along it. This, combined with the lofted nature of the mashie, and the fact that the ball dwells appreciably longer on the face of the club than if played direct, imparts both great back-spin to the ball and a certain amount of off-break. Balls thus played therefore invariably break to the right on pitching, and must therefore be deliberately and intentionally pitched to the left of the hole.

Now its dangers are manifold and obvious. There is little enough margin for error in meeting the ball directly, even though the club is travelling in the line of the proposed flight. But here the club is travelling obliquely; it brushes past the ball, and propels it with not the direct power of its stroke, but only the sideways push of it. If a driver were used in this manner with full swing, the result would be a slice of really historical value, but the comparative low velocity of the mashie-struck ball prevents this taking effect at all seriously, at any rate, in the air. On the other hand, the ball breaks to the right when once the more serious friction with the ground is established. On a soft green it seems to bite the ground as a blunt-nosed gimlet might. Then all its force is expended; it flops slowly a little to the right, and has no run in it. Like Sisera, where it falls there it falls down dead. Finally, it lies even deader than Sisera if the mashie is held very loose. Why this should be so is hard to say; it may have something to do with a check given to the free play of the wrists if the muscles of the fingers are taut. Mr. Horace Hutchinson parallels it—probably rightly—to the greater amount of side or break that can be put on to a billiard ball by holding the cue loosely. But it is a shot not recommended for parents and guardians.

Now though a quite full mashie shot—for reasons given above—is not recommended, it is probably easier to learn the amount of pull which it puts on than to learn how to play what is called a "spared" cleek shot. Sometimes the intuition comes, and the shot is successful; for intuition, meaning a feeling of certainty about a shot, is a prompting not to be disregarded, since the shot will be played with confidence. But in the general way there is nothing more difficult than to regulate the strength of driving clubs, namely, drivers, brassies, cleeks and driving irons. They are designed to hit as far as possible, and it is extremely difficult, at any rate without much practice, to play a half or a three-quarter cleek or brassie shot. It may come off, but for players of moderate calibre it probably will not; it is better for them to hit hard with a lofted iron or mashie than to play a sort of general stroke with a driving iron. The iron shot may be a little short, a yard or two from the edge of the green, but a " spared " shot with any driving club will (unless solid time is devoted to the practice of this stroke) probably not be so close.

But all this approaching, this play with irons and mashies may (for accidents will always occur) land one not on the green, where, as a matter of course, a putter is used, but just short of it, just to the side of it, or just beyond it. A dozen yards, or ten yards, or even two yards of stuff better avoided lie between the ball and the pleasant velvet, while not a dozen yards beyond lies the " haven where you would be." A couple of good putts—or one good putt and a " sitter "—would berth you if you were on the green, but you are not. *Que faire?*

Now it takes a very good putter indeed to hole out in two when ten yards of rough, and ten yards of green separate him from the hole. On the other hand, it does not entail a difficult or a fluky mashie shot to put the ball as near the hole from the same position, as a fine putter might reasonably hope to be if he putted from that distance. But the shot (though it sounds paradoxical) requires, from its very simplicity, some practice. Luckily the practice is not the least fatiguing, while, on the other hand, it is extremely paying. Probably in every round we play we have to make the decision as to whether we shall putt a ball through a little rough stuff or use a mashie. No doubt practice with a putter would lead to improvement, but beyond any doubt at all, practice with the mashie under such circumstances will lead to the same, and that to an extent undreamed of. This is especially the case in inland links, where the natural covering of the ground is not ideal golfing turf, and the green proper does not melt imperceptibly into the "through the green." In these inland courses very rough grass may often lie within a dozen yards of the hole. To putt through such is to bet against the inherent malignancy of inanimate objects. It is a bad bet, and it is much better to be safe in the air until they are left behind. Now whether a putter or mashie is used, allowance must be made for the run of the green, but on the whole there is more to be considered in a twenty yards putt than there is in a mashie-shot of the same length, for the putt is at the mercy of frictional obstacles all the way, whereas a mashie-shot is in the security of the air for some part of its course, and also a ball hit with a flat-faced putter is more liable to be turned out of its course by some one of these than that hit by a mashie. Only in these short mashie shots the stroke must be played quite simply. The ball—like every other ball—must be hit quite true, and the club must not be checked. Any attempt to pitch it near the hole with cut to stop it is wholly unnecessary, and may be most disastrous. It has to be pitched on the green and it will run. The ball itself is quite as easy to hit true as is a putt of the same length. There is nothing simpler in the whole of golf than this stroke, yet it is often foozled for two reasons; the first that some men will play it with a jerk (the same play stymies with a jerk, and usually put the other ball in), the second, that people will take their eye off the ball in order to see how close to the hole it is going before they have hit it. Now in these very short and easy shots it is well to stand open to the hole, and to keep the body quite rigid as in putting. This is best achieved by playing the ball off the right leg, with it nearly opposite to the right foot. There is thus less temptation to play tricks, to attempt to cut the ball, etc., and it makes the stroke look easy, which it is. More especially this mashie-shot is easier than the corresponding putt would be, if it is made down hill, for the slight inevitable drag put on the ball by the mashie is a special Providence to check it for a moment as it pitches, let it recollect itself, and roll slowly.

The stroke itself is so simple as to be almost indescribable, while the corresponding putt is so difficult as to be quite indescribable. There is no question of pitching the ball high; it has to be lobbed over the rough, pitched on the green, and run. But it must be played with definite intention; the ball must be designed to pitch within an area of a couple of yards or so. Given the lie in the rough is good, it is probably easy (with practice) to do this from a distance of ten yards; given the lie is bad, it is only lunatics—there are plenty of them—who would take a putter. The stroke has to be lobbed, *without any cut;* but, after a look at the lie of the green, the definite intention of where it is meant to pitch is essential. Finally, any attempt to look up before the ball is struck is especially deprecated.

But the most distant green is reached at last, and then the struggle begins all over again. If it were not that we knew, we parents and guardians, by long and bitter experience, how often we took three on the green from the distance of twenty yards, we should have thought it impossible to be such villainous performers. But we may remember for our comfort that the man who never takes more than two putts from a distance of twenty yards has happily yet to be born. When he is born he will sweep the board. And also we may remember that however good your approach-work is, yet if you only average thirty-six putts on a round you are a very good putter indeed. For every fault which it is possible to make in all the rest of golf put together we all constantly make in the putting green. We putt, we slice, we top, we jerk, we omit the follow-through, we hit the ground, we take our eyes off the ball, we pull our arms in, we misjudge distance, even if it is a matter of a few yards only. We most of us typify, in fact, in a single round, on the putting green, every fault known to man. And the maddening part of this whole distressing business is that we have only got to hit straight, with the most elementary sense of strength (except in a few greens like the 12th at Ashdown Forest, where the Lord only knows what may happen), and we shall at any rate get down in two, and join the thin rank of first-rate putters. Often our faults do not completely find us out ; in a putt of a yard, for instance, we often putt execrably and yet go down. But supposing we commit the same idiocy in a putt of four yards, it may easily take us three to hole out. How mortal man can fail to putt out a ball at the distance of a yard is indiscoverable. But since immortal golfers do so fail, the cause of so unspeakable an aberration must be examined.

Now, on a small scale, the same fault which in driving will produce a prodigious slice, will in a two-yard putt produce a slice of about two inches. But this is sufficient to leave the hole untenanted. Therefore, when we are putting we must not slice, we must not turn the toe of the putter out, or drag it across the ball, nor must we stand with our right foot too far advanced, unless this happens to be an entirely successful method with us, for it naturally leads to slicing. In the same way we must not pull, or we shall go to the left of the hole, or hit the ball on the top, or hit the ground instead of it—a fault which we all persistently commit. Nor, above all, must we take our eye off the ball, even if we are within two feet of the hole.

Putting then, it would appear, is as difficult as driving. It is much more so. A far greater proportion of people are good drivers than good putters, since not only is every possible fault in driving possible in putting, but because in putting an estimate of requisite strength is necessary. And to estimate strength in this delicate operation *quite exactly*, we have to judge of the wind, which, absurd as it may sound, affects putting enormously, and one has on most greens to see how the grass is cut, and which way it grows. Supposing, for instance, your ball lies on one of those parallels of smoothed grass down which the mowing machine has lately passed, smoothing all the grass between you and the hole one way, it will make a very appreciable difference in the run of your ball if every blade is smoothed towards the hole or away from the hole. But we are not yet good enough putters to attend to things like these, though the difference they make to a putt is great. Instead let us be up.

Now this eternal advice has more than one thing to recommend it. It is obviously true that if we are not up we shall not be in, whereas if we are, we possibly may. But in addition to this, we all instinctively underestimate the effect of the constant friction of the grass on a putted ball. It may be that we are accustomed to see balls start in the air from every other club (provided we hit them properly), and be uninterfered with till later on in their chequered career, whereas a putt has pitched, so to speak, from the moment of its start. *Ceteris paribus*, it is as easy or as difficult to get into a hole from a yard beyond it as from a yard this side of it. But if we studiously prefer to play a yard this side of it we miss a certain percentage (for every one putts straight occasionally) of balls which would have gone in.

Now the modes of putting are as the sand of the sea; one man crouches as if there were Boers behind a neighbouring kopje; one stands on his left leg, another on his right; one taps the ball as if it were a friend's shoulder, another as if it were a wasp to be killed; one uses a wooden putter; another, some patent abortion; a third, an iron putter; a fourth, a debilitated cleek; a fifth, a Dutch hoe; a sixth, a sort of stone breaker; a seventh, a kind of steel tobacco pipe. All these may be first-class putters. The point is that we are not even second-rate, and no Dutch tobacco pipes, *per se*, will probably help us. But whatever instrument or attitude first putters use, they will have certain things in common, certain other things which they, being persons of genius, may employ, but which we, being nothing of the kind, had better discard. With regard to putting, then, for you and I are execrable putters, we had better begin from the beginning. The ball is, after various vicissitudes on the green, not more than ten yards from the hole; the opponent's ball is at about the same distance from the hole. We are all square, and there are two thousand holes yet to play. In other words, there is at present no emergency of any kind; we want to putt reasonably throughout the two thousand holes. What is to be done?

In the first place go to the opposite side of the hole and look at the apparent line of the hole from your ball to it. You will see a certain lie of the ground, bearing to the right or left, or up hill or down hill, unless it appears to you that the green is absolutely level. If so, it was quite worth examination, for it is a priceless discovery. Next (without unduly wasting time) have a glance at the hole from a yard or two behind your ball. You will probably find that your estimate made from the other side of the hole was the correct one. If not, you will be wise to trust to what you have seen from beyond the hole. Here etiquette comes in : do not be a nuisance ; on the other hand, you have a right to give yourself the best chance. So if you are honestly not satisfied with these two observations, take them again. Then without further expenditure of time take your putter, and remember that having taken your observations, no putt gets easier by being looked at. In fact it gets more shy, more self-conscious. Then ground your club with the full weight of the club immediately behind the ball, and *visualize* a ball going to the hole from the position in which your ball lies; imagine, that is to say, a ball which goes (not near, but) into the hole, starting from the position in which you are now. If it suits your fancy, look at a particular blade of grass over which it will pass, and lay your putter at right angles to it. If not, merely lay your putter at right angles to the first six inches of the proposed route. You will then almost certainly find that the centre of the putter is not opposite to the centre of your ball. Correct this. Then estimate the quality of the ground you have to pass over, and determine the force with which you will have to hit (if you prefer that), or the distance to which you must withdraw the putter to get the necessary strength to *reach* the hole. Then stand absolutely rigid, and say to yourself, "I will hit so hard that it will gobble in. I will hit harder than is necessary, and I will hit it quite true." And then, if God is good, and you have said this very determinedly, you may just be up and in. But if you are not quite determined to be beyond the hole you will certainly not get there.

About the proper stance we have said nothing, since there is no proper stance. As long as the putter is drawn back quite straight (not rather straight, in which case it will slice or pull one inch or two or three, and all your four-foot putts will be missed), it does not matter how you stand as long as you are quite comfortable and your body is quite rigid. The point is that the putter should meet the ball absolutely square, and that the ball should be hit neither low nor high. Thus the attitude suggested, *i.e.*, standing on the right leg with the ball opposite the right foot is only a suggestion, made in case it has not yet been tried by the reader. It seems at any rate an attitude which is comfortable, and does not predispose to any huge mis-hit of the ball.

Putting is an operation at which, with all of us, there is a great deal of room for improvement. But very few consistently improve. An ordinarily poor putter may putt much better than is his wont for a day, or a week, or even a month, but then will probably fall back again. But while he is putting comparatively well, he seldom takes the trouble to observe himself, and see in what his attitude, grip of the club, manner of studying his putt has differed from his ordinary performance. Few people practise putting, because they say it is "no good." They are quite right; it is no good practising in the way they would probably practise, *i.e.*, tumbling six balls on to the green and hitting them anyhow, one with the toe, one with the heel, and one with the centre of the putter. But it would be of the utmost use if the same man set about his practice intelligently, and the following is given as a possible suggestion. Go with a few balls, not to a difficult green full of undulations, but to a green as nearly flat as possible, for the initial difficulties of hitting the ball true must be overcome before the question is complicated by considerations of slope, and lay yourself a perfectly simple putt of about ten feet. Look at it carefully, putt it carefully, and observe the result without moving your feet from where they have been. The ball, in all probability, will be to the right of the hole (unless you have got it in), and not up. If so, and you are satisfied you hit the ball square and in the centre of the blade, keep your left foot exactly where it is, draw back the right an inch or two, and putt again in as nearly as possible the same manner as before. If you succeed in doing this you will almost certainly find that the ball will not go so much to the right. If, on the other hand, you find that the first ball has gone to the left of the hole, advance your right foot an inch or two. It is very hard to make people believe that stance can have anything to do with putting. They tell you scornfully, "If you putt straight it will go in." That is undeniably true, but then, since for the most part we do not putt straight, it is conceivably worth while trying to find out why we putt crooked. And the stance has as much to do with putting as it has with driving. No doubt many people drive very open and drive straight, putt very open and putt straight; but in driving, if you find you consistently drive to the right of the line, you will be wise to draw back your right foot a little. So also in putting; if you find that you consistently putt to the right of the hole, make the same alteration. All our calculations on putting, such as they are, are based on the assumption that we are going to hit the ball true. To do this it must be hit with the middle of the putter (unless there is a special reason for doing otherwise), the putter must meet the ball square, and it must not be checked till the ball has left it. These rules are golden. It is worth while, therefore, for those who generally do not hit the ball in the middle of the putter to have a nick made in the middle of its upper edge, which they can deliberately lay opposite the centre of the ball when they address it. It will not make them always hit the ball in the centre of the putter, but they have a far better chance of doing it if, anyhow, when the ball is addressed, the putter is in the right position. Then let them imagine a line drawn from the hole to the ball, and lay the putter at right angles to it when they address the ball. This, again, gives them the chance of hitting the ball square; and, finally, let them follow through with every putt, even the shortest. They will thus run less risk of checking the club before the ball is really hit, and will then have a chance of going more than half-way. Even that is something on some days.

Now, apart from the correct striking of the ball, good putters putt in two widely different manners. Some look at the hole, imagine their line, and putt as far as possible along it; others select a particular blade of grass on that line and somewhere near their ball, and putt (as far as possible) over that, disregarding the hole altogether, except in so far as it is a question of strength to get there. Personally, we cannot see that one has any very great advantage over the other. No doubt if one dismisses the hole altogether (except in so far as it concerns strength), there is less tendency to look up at the last moment at the hole. On the other hand, is there not a corresponding tendency at the last moment to look up at that favoured blade of grass? However, both methods are certainly consistent with good putting, and one of the two is essential to it.

Having therefore—after, who knows how much practice on a level green?—got into a habit of hitting the ball with the middle of the putter, not with the toe, and of laying the putter at right angles to the proposed line, and of being beyond the hole rather than short of it, it will be time to see what can be done on a more difficult green. To this more difficult green it is necessary to carry everything that has been learned. However wavy the green, from whatever height above the hole or depth below it you have to putt, it is still always better to go on hitting the ball clean, and not attempt any tricks about giving it drag or counter-acting the natural curl of the green by unnaturally putting slice on to your putt. Only one possible exception to what has already been said occurs to us, and that is when one is lying below the hole on a steep green. Then, and then only, is it wiser to be a little short than a little too far, since a down hill putt of whatever length is always harder than an up-hill putt of the same length, since from above the hole in a short putt the ball must be started slow, and is then more at the mercy of any irregularity on the green than one which may be hit fairly from below the hole. On the irregular and wavy green, in fact, the putt itself must be made in exactly the same manner as on the flat green; but before putting one has to settle one's estimate of how far the roll of the green will make the ball curve in its course, what extra strength will be required to get it up a hill, and how far its roll, when once it is started, will take it down hill.

Now the same people who will not practise on a level green will equally refuse to practise on a curly one. They will (again scornfully) tell you that any amount of practice on any green will only teach you the peculiarities of that green. This is not in the least true, and one might as well say that the study of Plato would only teach one Plato, and not Greek. For the effect of slope on a ball on one green, though it may not be identical with the effect of slope on another (owing to differences of turf, etc.), will very closely resemble it, and intelligent practice on any curly green will help you to a knowledge of that elusive genus, not only of that elusive specimen. You will notice also that on a green heavy with rain or thick with grass the sideways slope of the ground will tell on your ball much less than when it is dry or is very close-cropped, and thus you will learn to allow less for sideways slope in wet weather than in dry. You will also learn that a putt slows down quicker in the last yards or so of its course when going up hill than you could ever have guessed, and that it retains its original impetus far longer than you would have guessed, until you patiently observe, when going down hill. You will learn also that a slope on the green to a sliced putt is like a wind from the left to a sliced drive, and that it accentuates your error enormously. And if you will, you can profit by the knowledge. But above all, as in mashie-play, so in putting give up any idea of "general" putts that may do something. In so precise and delicate an operation "general" shots end in disaster. The problem of how to get to the hole may be a very difficult one. But make as good a conjecture as you possibly can about it, and try to put that conjecture into practice. Never say to yourself, "It is a pure fluke whether I get near the hole or not." Very likely according to your present methods it may be, but try to let it cease to be a fluke.

CHAPTER III.

EXERCISES.

It is perfectly true that the possession of very great physical strength is not at all a primary necessity for the golfer, except sometimes in the use of the niblick, when a couple of inches of sand has to be exploded into the air, or a piece of a furze-bush demolished as a preliminary to moving the ball at all. At the same time most really long drivers are men of good muscle, and physical strength is throughout the game an advantage, not because one puts it all into requisition, but because one does not.

This sounds at first a paradox, but in other and less paradoxical form what it amounts to is that the physically powerful man is playing well within himself, while a weaker man has to approach much nearer to the limits of his strength thus, taxing his muscles and sooner tiring them. Now using the muscles to their utmost is known as "pressing," and, on the whole, parents and guardians are recommended not to press. Within certain limits, of course, everyone uses muscles, or else the club could never stir at all; but it is important to keep to certain limits—*i.e.*, never, except very occasionally, to demand from the muscles their full strength. Also, it is particularly important to give to the muscles the right kind of strength, which in golf means not the power of slowly overcoming a large inertia, but the power of quickly and accurately imparting speed to the club. The muscles, therefore, should not be ponderous, but speedy workers.

There is then, what, for the purposes of golf, we may call the wrong sort of strength, and this is the sort of strength which is produced by weight-lifting, dumb-bell exercises and gymnastics, in which the arms are used to support and move the weight of the body. In this connection it is interesting to see that Lieut. F. G. Tait found that his course of gymnastic instruction, while it increased his strength, yet shortened his drive. This is exactly what one would expect. For the practice of dumb-bells and gymnastics has as its object the acquisition of strength which is meant to bear sustained efforts, and overcome the inertia of heavy bodies, and though, no doubt, muscles may be simultaneously trained to acquire speed as well, it must be understood that the mere acquisition of a more powerful arm or shoulder does not in the least imply that one's driving capacity will be increased. Indeed, the opposite is probably nearer the case, for dumb-bell exercise induces a slow, though powerful action of the muscles, which, as a habit, is more than likely to make them lose their habit of speed. The muscles necessary are of a different breed; it would be as reasonable to expect a cart-horse to win the Derby owing to its huge muscles, as to expect a professional strong man to drive a long ball by reason of his strength. His muscles, of course, may also have been trained to speed, but his dumb-bell exercises have not helped him to that.

Exercises for golf, then, designed to increase the speed of the muscles, and to cultivate the habit of accuracy, must not be devised on these lines. Dumb-bells and such things, it is true, may easily form a valuable supplement, as likely to give additional strength to an abnormally weak muscle, but that modicum of strength once acquired, they have done their work. These exercises also (in fact, for our immediate purpose this is their main object) should enable a man who plays only at irregular intervals to resume his game, after a fortnight or a month of total abstinence, without feeling stiff and tied up. It is quite possible that for a hole or two his eye, unaccustomed to judge distances, may estimate the length of ball required wrongly, but apart from this he ought to fall into his regular game anyhow at once, not shuffle on his feet in taking his stance, and feel uncomfortable when he has taken it; not raise his eye from the unstruck ball oftener than usual; not slice more pointedly than is his wont; not putt very wide from the hole. More than this it is, we believe, easily possible that he will find, if he has been a little diligent at some of these exercises, that his game has definitely improved since the time he saw a golf link last. He will be standing to address his ball more comfortably than he used, and he will hit it with greater accuracy. These exercises, it may be at once stated, are quite dull, but not duller than dumb-bells; they are also strictly intended only for those who are indifferent performers, but seriously desire to be different.

Now in all shots of whatever kind in golf, distance and direction are the two things and the two things only desirable. For distance speed of muscle is required, for direction accuracy of striking. Accuracy and speed, then, are the objects of these exercises, and as a corollary, which will come of itself, facility. This, perhaps, is as important as either, for from facility comes confidence.

Take, then, a thick piece of baize, about four feet square, and tack it loosely down to prevent it wrinkling over the carpet or on the boards of any room. Then remove in every direction within the possible radius of the club you propose to use, all perishable objects. Stand on the baize firmly, as if addressing a ball on the tee, waggling your driver at some rolled-up scrap of paper which you have placed there, till you are as certain as a man can be that you have got your distance right, that your stance is quite comfortable, and that you would wager a reasonable sum that given there was a golf-ball where the paper is, you would drive it with fair correctness. Then, without moving your feet, outline their position with chalk, and mark where the ball is supposed to be. Then take your ordinary swing and try to hit the paper. Most parents and guardians will not succeed in doing so ; their clubs will either hiss innocuously over it, or else deal the baize a somewhat severe blow some inches from where the paper lay. More especially will they fail to hit it, if they press at all, for the object aimed at is perhaps not a third the size of a golf-ball, and instead of being teed sits down on the green baize. Let them, however, with all the concentration they can command, take three or four more shots at it.

Now this sort of practice is evidently much more difficult than the problem of hitting a ball on the tee. That is exactly the reason why it is recommended. For half-a-dozen shots you may easily miss the paper altogether, in which case a slight variation of stance is recommended, but the patient parent is here solemnly assured that he very soon will hit the paper, and that after he has hit it once he will very soon begin to hit it in the majority of instances that he tries. Supposing he finds his original stance was not right, he must mark out the position in which he finds he can hit it with ease and comfort, and rest assured that it is almost certainly his right stance. He may, if he wishes, recommend the same to a friend, but there is no reason to suppose it is his friend's right stance.

Supposing, therefore, that you have a month's, or even only a week's forced abstention from golf, and during that time you have on, say, six days out of seven taken the trouble to address the piece of paper from your correct stance and swing at it half-a-dozen times, you may without undue sanguineness expect to find yourself addressing the real ball on the real tee, if when you next play with a confidence and a comfortableness that you are not accustomed to. If there is anything in practice this must be so. Daily you have taken up your right stance, and never have you taken up a wrong stance. It is reasonable, therefore, to expect that you have at any rate begun to form the habit of taking up the right stance instinctively, and have begun to break with the habit of shuffling and uncertainty on the tee, a fault almost ineradicable with mediocre and irregular players.

Now on this same piece of baize draw a straight chalk line through the place marked for the ball, and in the direction of the supposed line of the hole, for the distance of a foot or two both behind and in front of the place where the ball lies. Swing quite slowly up and down, stopping the club at the moment it reaches the place where the ball is supposed to be. Look carefully at the angle the club makes with the chalk line. It ought to be at right angles to it. If it is not, there is some correction to be made, either in the grip, or (which is less likely if the stance is really comfortable) in the stance, or in even so slow a swing as this. What the correction is, it is impossible for the writer to say, but in any case it is infinitely easier for the practiser to find out at ease in his house, than it would be in the middle of a match.

But perhaps it is in putting (also dull) that you will find most correction is necessary. Here the position of the feet for the driving stance should be entirely disregarded, and the attention for the present entirely devoted to the white line. The centre of the putter (for those who putt inaccurately) must be laid at right angles across the white line. Take the putter in your ordinary grip, and putt gently at an imaginary ball, looking to see if the putter moves straight up and down the white line. It almost certainly will not. But it has to, for the whole essence of putting is that it should meet the ball square at right angles to the line of the hole. But unless you are a good putter, the club will want to go almost anywhere else, either because you pull your arms in, or because you push them out, or because you are standing wrong. And the right stance in putting for every individual player is that in which his putter moves naturally over this line. With a little shifting of the feet (when you are satisfied that you are not pulling your arms in or pushing them out) you will soon arrive at some position of the feet in which the putter moves naturally up and down the line to the hole. If you feel comfortable in that position, mark the places occupied by the feet with extreme care. If you do not, try another. But if you do, move quite away, come back again, replace the feet, and again swing the putter over the line. Repeat this once or twice, and if you find that each time the centre of the putter swings naturally down the line, you may feel pretty sure that that position is right for you. The point, therefore, is to remember that position by making a habit of it, and if every day for a week in which you do not play golf, you take up that marked position a dozen times and play a dozen imaginary putts from it, you will find that, dull and ridiculous and childish as the practice seems, it will make you feel more comfortable when you return to the green, and that your putter will in a greater number of cases than before send the ball comparatively straight. The club in practice should be made to " whisper " over the place where the ball is supposed to be, and be neither passed over it in the air, nor dragged along the baize. This will tend to make you hit the ball pretty well in the centre, instead of hitting it on the top, or merely, as we all do sometimes, digging jerkily into the green.

It has been seen in an earlier part of this book that James Braid attributes the exceptional length of his drives to the use of his wrists, which are exceptionally strong, while later it has been noticed that it is mainly by their use that approach shots are so cut as to be nearly dead on pitching. It is evident, then, since so high an authority as Braid assigns to them so important a work, that speed of movement in the wrists is worth cultivation. For most moderate golfers find great difficulty in making this movement fast, and yet keeping the stroke accurate, with the result that they either give up the attempt altogether, or content themselves with erratic, if occasionally long results.

Now whenever the wrists are used in a

stroke at golf it is clear that the right wrist makes a forehand stroke, the left a backhand stroke. These two have to be timed together ; neither should pull the other, and the practiser should begin, not by attempting to put wrist into a full swing, but holding the driver over the putting line and addressing the mark where the ball is supposed to be, without moving his arms, bring the club back as far as his wrists will let him, and make a wrist-flick only with it, bringing it forward to the full extent of the wrists with the utmost possible speed. Here the beginner will at first utterly fail to keep the club-head in anything like the right line ; he will cross it from left to right and right to left with the most devious inaccuracy, as one wrist overpulls the other. But the correct movement is immensely well worth attaining, and when thoroughly attained, when, that is to say, the club is made to move really fast on its right line, it should be combined with the ordinary swing, the wrists being turned over in the manner which Braid describes so very clearly, and only flicked forward when the club is close to the ball. It is there that their force should be used, the common fault being to begin to use the wrists far sooner than is right, with the effect that probably an inaccurate stroke is made, and that certainly their little best is spent before the ball is struck. This use of the wrists is an affair of considerable delicacy, and it would be hopeless for a man who has habitually not used them or used them incorrectly, to attempt to incorporate them straight away into the full shot. But by beginning with the simple movement of them alone, and afterwards combining them with the swing, we believe that the attainment is not very difficult.

Finally, this dull business of a chalked line and chalked foot-marks is valuable for the correction of any error, because when nothing depends on the stroke much more attention can be given to method than when a hole and even a match hangs on it. It is said there are forty-two distinct things to be thought of in driving, but woe to the man who consciously thinks of them when he is addressing his ball! But in privacy, when no ball is there, and no one is the worse for a missed shot or two, one can much more consciously and thoroughly devote one's mind to the method of the thing. A good eye is not a gift that can be bought this way, but a correct application of acquired knowledge can. But it is dull: there is no getting over that, and being dull it is only recommended for those parents and guardians who take their game really seriously.

The two or three exercises here given are only meant to be examples of a hundred that can be used with advantage in the practice without a ball. But the one thing needful is that the practiser should know what he wants to practise: given he knows an error into which he falls and the way to correct it, or given he knows how to play a particular shot and wishes to practise it, he will certainly get to learn it quicker by a dozen carefully-played shots a day in his room than by a couple of wild strokes in a round at the game itself. Many people also have found that a long looking-glass placed opposite them assists in detecting errors.

But above all, never practise vaguely, like the man who plays a dozen "general" mashie shots on to the green. It is no use whatever to wildly swoop a club over a piece of baize, standing wrong, holding the club wrong, doing everything wrong except by accident. That sort of practice has an effect, no doubt, as all practice has, but its particular effect is to ingrain and confirm existing errors. In most of us they are sufficiently ingrained already; it is superfluous to practise them further.

Part V.

―――

American Balls and English Players

BY

C. L.

AMERICAN BALLS AND ENGLISH PLAYERS.

THERE has been a great deal of discussion, mostly acrimonious, of late about the last improvement made in balls. For years the gutty has held the monopoly, but now a far better ball, namely the American rubber-filled, has been introduced, and has been met with a warm welcome on the one hand, on the other with shrill abuse.

But now one may reasonably hope that all the unwise and unpleasant things that were to be said about it have been said, and it remains only to express a pious wish that this regrettable discussion is closed. For what happened? A vastly superior article appeared, and certain leading golfers found that their inferior brethren were able to improve their length of drive and get with less difficulty out of difficulties than they had hitherto been able. Drivers, whose carry was wont to fail before reaching places of safety, sailed securely over, and greens which were out of reach to others became negotiable in one. That, when all is said and done, was the root of their objections, and on this score it was said that the American ball "spoiled" certain famous holes at famous links, by shortening, practically speaking, their length. Now it is not very many years ago that the gutty was a new-comer. Once golfers used to use a ball made of compressed feathers; then came the gutty (eventually nicked), which reduced the exceptional carry to an easy carry, and put hole after hole which could in the old days be only reached in two shots or three within reach of one shot or two. The gutty in fact "spoiled" myriads of holes in the same way exactly as the rubber-filled ball is "spoiling" them now. If then this outcry—happily dying away—about the American ball is justified, we should in strict logic discard the gutty also, and go back to the feather-filled ball, or, if Mr. Andrew Lang can inform us on the subject, to its predecessor.

Golf in its very essence is a game which anyone may play with what instruments he pleases, given that explosives, machinery and outside agencies are not employed to propel the ball. It has to be struck, and the driving force has to be the human frame. What has to be struck is any object whatsoever. A man may play with a billiard ball, a football, a cricket ball, a tennis ball. As a matter of fact he (till a year or so ago), generally played with a gutty ball because it went farther than any other variety of ball. Before that he played with a feather ball for the same reason. And for the same reason he now plays with a rubber-filled ball. That ball was invented and patented in America. But supposing it had been invented and patented in England, has it not occurred to anybody that *perhaps* there would not have been quite so much adverse criticism of it? Everyone will certainly shout "No." Afterwards perhaps they will begin to wonder.

But apart from this the main outcry has really been that it puts the shorter driver, if he uses an American ball, as far as driving goes, on a level with a rather longer driver if he uses a gutty ball. The remedy, it appears then, is entirely in the hands of the rather longer driver. But some of them refused to take it; they continued to use gutties, and said it was "not fair." But why they continue to use gutties, is, I think, sufficiently obvious. For the American ball, except in practised hands, is more difficult to deal with in short shots and on the green. At first every-one—except bad players, who did not notice much difference—found that it was not quite so easy to drop it dead in a mashie-shot, without run, as a gutty, and that it exhibited a liveliness to them uncontroll-able under the putter. So it was "not fair."

Golf is an old game, but it is still just possible that all improvements in its instru-ments are not yet made. Whether there was an outcry or not against the intro-duction of the gutty ball by the feather-players, I do not know. It is extremely probable. If there was not, it shows the greater good sense of golfers of that day; if there was, time has now shown how futile their outcry was, and our own good sense shows us how futile it must have been. In ten years, time and the good sense of players of that day will see how futile the present outcry has been.

Another objection made against the American ball was its expensiveness. That the initial cost of it is greater is perfectly true, but it is now proved beyond doubt, that it lasts far longer than the gutty, and that in spite of its initial expense it is for the majority of players, those in fact who constantly top their balls, a cheaper ball to play with. A good Kempshall or Haskell, habitually topped, will play its half-dozen rounds with cheerfulness, and after a bit of paint be as good as new. Besides, a feather ball, which could not be topped without disaster (that was why irons, cleeks, mashies appeared with the gutty), cost twice as much as a rubber ball. Yet the expense of the feather ball was not at that time considered to "spoil" the game.

It is probably true that an extremely long driver does not get much additional length off the tee by using a rubber ball. It will be demonstrated why some day (and disproved the next), but that at present is the verdict of very long drivers. But the facility of getting out of bad lies (even a very long driver has occasionally a bad lie) is his, and his also is the difficulty which his inferior antagonist encounters on nearing the green. The American ball has been supposed to "neutralize skill"; it is therefore the mission of the skilful to show that this is not so. At most holes they have an opportunity of doing it. Finally, the American ball is more fun. Anyone who has played with it knows exactly what this means. And those who have not have no right to express an opinion.

C. L.

THE END.

Breinigsville, PA USA
02 December 2009
228515BV00003B/97/A